E AN ESL READERS S

Third Edition

Follows: Lesson 4

Reader: The Neighborhood Laundromatte

THIRD · EDITION

ENCOUNTERS

AN · ESL · READER

PAUL PIMSLEUR

Late of the State University of New York, Albany

DONALD BERGER

BEVERLY PIMSLEUR

Harcourt Brace & Company

Orlando   San Diego   New York
Toronto   London   Sydney   Tokyo

456789 043 98

ISBN: 0-15-522600-2
Library of Congress Catalog Card Number: 85-80868
Printed in the United States of America

Drawings by Ed Malsberg
Copyrights and Acknowledgments and Photo Credits appear on pages
219-20, which constitute a continuation of the copyright page.

Preface

The Third Edition of *Encounters: An ESL Reader,* by Beverly Pimsleur and Donald Berger, maintains the learning concept originally developed by the late Paul Pimsleur. As described in the preface to the first edition, *Encounters* is

> a book of journalistic articles, simplified and arranged for students desiring to improve their reading of English. The aim is to familiarize students with American magazines and newspapers, and to help them progress step by step toward reading fluently.
>
> The vocabulary consists of some 1500 basic words, with the less common words defined in the margins. Exercises following the articles stress vocabulary, grammar, and comprehension. Our intention is to encourage students to know more, not just about the English language but about interesting or unusual aspects of life in North America.

As in previous editions, *Encounters* is a graded reader based on articles from current periodicals; this edition has been completely updated to reflect new dimensions in American culture and pedagogy. A new type of exercise, Sequencing, has been added to the wealth of vocabulary, grammar, and comprehension exercises. Increased attention has been given to role playing and paired practice exercises, and to topics for class discussion. In addition, special dictation exercises have been prepared and are included in the Instructor's Manual.

We would like to thank Al Richards, our acquisitions editor at Harcourt Brace Jovanovich, for his continuing help and advice in the preparation of this edition. Thanks also to the National Theatre of the Deaf and the staff of the Cherry Blossom Festival for their contributions. Our special thanks go to Cate Safranek, Maggie Porter, and Dean Reed of Harcourt Brace Jovanovich for their conscientious and careful work.

Beverly Pimsleur
Donald Berger

Contents

Introduction

The selections in this book are drawn from magazines and newspapers like *The New Yorker* and *The Boston Globe.* They are adapted to meet space and vocabulary restrictions, and to maintain a gradation of difficulty from the beginning of the book to the end. In every case, we have tried to keep the style and spirit of the original articles alive, so that they will be as interesting to new readers as they were to us when we first read them.

In short, students will find here the kind of reading matter they might encounter daily—the kind they would want to read for their own information and enjoyment—but simplified to the point where they can truly *read* and not merely decipher it.

Gradation

Reading with understanding depends on the interplay of three factors: vocabulary, structure (grammar), and meaning. If the meaning of a sentence is obvious, most students will understand it in spite of a difficult word or structure; if the meaning is unclear, even knowing all the words and structures may not suffice to interpret it.

In sequencing the articles in this book, we have tried to control this three-fold measure of difficulty. We assume from the outset that students are at least somewhat familiar with a basic vocabulary, and that they have covered in class the chief grammatical structures of English. Having learned these words and structures one by one from a textbook, they are now ready for the next step in learning to read: encountering them in real life. The earliest articles in this book are the simplest ones; they gradually grow more complex in vocabulary, structure, and meaning, but with an attempt to compensate for any special difficulty in one area by simplicity in the others. Our point is to give students extensive practice in understanding natural English prose, at a rate of difficulty that will challenge but not overwhelm them.

Vocabulary

The basic vocabulary of *Encounters* consists of approximately 1500 high-utility words.* A certain number of other words also appear, but these are limited to no more than one new word in thirty-five familiar ones. Students should be able to read several lines, picking up speed and fluency, before they encounter an unknown word. Once introduced, a new word generally recurs several times, in different contexts, to help ensure retention.

Exercises

The exercises are designed to channel the students' enthusiasm into useful language-learning activities. Some exercises reinforce points of vocabulary and grammar; others challenge the students to answer questions and to express views. The exercises are brief and varied, so as not to risk dulling the students' zest for reading.

Vocabulary Exercises

At least two vocabulary exercises appear after each story, using such techniques as requiring definitions using words from the story ("Golf and baseball are both popular *sports* in America.") In most cases, the students should supply the missing words or phrase from memory. It is best to go on to the next item if the answer cannot be found quickly.

In responding, the student should say the whole sentence, not just the missing word. The instructor should insist on accurate pronunciation, modeling the pronunciation for the class when necessary. Choral (whole-class) and individual repetition are both valuable in exercising pronunciation.

Grammar Exercises

Two or more grammatical exercises called *Structures* follow each article. These are "pattern drills." They progress in difficulty during the course of the book and touch upon many im-

---

* The basic vocabulary, with which students are assumed to be familiar, is taken from words with the highest frequencies in lists found in: Michael P. West and James G. Endicott, *The New Method English Dictionary,* 4th ed. (London: Longman Group Ltd., 1961); John B. Carroll, Peter Davies, and Barry Richman, *The American Heritage Word Frequency Book* (Boston: Houghton Mifflin Co., 1971); and John R. Shaw and Janet Shaw, *The New Horizon Ladder Dictionary of the English Language* (New York: New American Library, 1970).

portant points of English grammar. An exercise from an article on the golfer Nancy Lopez will illustrate how they can be used.

C   She practices each day.   →   **She keeps on practicing each day.**

1.   She smiles during the game.
2.   She improves each year.
3.   She plays in every tournament.
4.   She follows her parents.

To begin, the instructor says the model stimulus and response several times, at normal speed, both to show the students what to do, and to model the correct intonation. Then the instructor says the stimulus alone ("She practices each day.") and indicates by a gesture that all the students are to respond, in chorus ("She keeps on practicing each day."). The instructor then says sentence one ("She smiles during the game.") and waits for a choral response from the class ("She keeps on smiling during the game."). The correct response is confirmed by repeating it after the students. If the drill proves easy, the instructor may call on individuals to respond to the remaining sentences; if it is difficult, the choral work may be continued, giving the class added practice. The drill can be lengthened by reusing the same sentences in random order. As a final step, the instructor might go through it a second time, having individual students say the stimuli and the responses.

It is possible to do these drills in writing, and even to use them as tests, but it is important to first do them aloud quite thoroughly, so that the grammatical point is mastered by sound as well as by sight.

Paired Practice

Many of the grammar exercises are designed for two students at a time. This use of paired practice, and similar group work, has long been shown to have sound pedagogical and linguistic value. Among other things, such practice increases the students' ability to use English, and motivates students by involving them in their lessons at a more personal level.

Instructors are encouraged to use the paired-practice approach often, in the exercises where it is specifically called for and in others whenever it is felt to be appropriate.

Comprehension Exercises

The easiest of the comprehension exercises are those called *True or False*. These consist of statements about the article, some true, some not. If a statement is true, students should repeat it aloud, possibly prefacing it with an expression of agreement like "That's true," or "That's right." If the statement is false, they should make whatever changes are necessary to make it true. This type of exercise is meant to be easy enough so that all students can participate in it successfully.

Next in difficulty are the *Questions* found after every article. They test the students' understanding of the article's main ideas, rather than its details. Students should be encouraged to attempt the fullest answers they feel capable of expressing, and to give natural answers, substituting pronouns for nouns, for example.

The most challenging exercises appear under the headings *Points of View, Discussion,* and *Imagination.* Here, the students are invited to express their own views on topics suggested by the article. These exercises often elicit lively classroom discussion. Later, after the discussion has helped the students to formulate their ideas, these topics can be assigned as compositions.

A special category of exercises called *Cross-Cultural Topics* invites comparisons between life styles in various parts of America and/or other parts of the world. These are always placed last and may be omitted if they are inappropriate.

Dictation Exercises

Dictation exercises are very helpful in giving students practice in writing. These exercises, however, appear only in the Instructor's Manual. The instructor may omit any of these or may add other dictation exercises taken word for word from the articles, or with minor changes, as desired.

Dictations should be scheduled for a time after the students have become quite familiar with the article and have completed most or all of the accompanying exercises.

Teaching Suggestions

Prereading

It is often helpful to prepare the students for the article they are about to read. Instructors, speaking from their own experiences, can offer some details about the magazine, the topic, or the circumstances surrounding the article. They can also present words and constructions that the students may have difficulty in reading, by making up examples that are similar, but not identical, to the difficult ones. Further, they can focus the students' attention and help them to read with a purpose by asking in advance two or three questions to which the students are to find the answers in the article.

Reading is usually done silently, as a form of covert speech, and the instructor needs to make certain that the sounds the students make while reading silently are correct ones. If not, poor speech habits may be reinforced. Learning the mechanics of reading includes:

Mechanics
of Reading

• acquiring the habit of making accurate correspondences between sounds and printed letters

• learning to read in meaningful thought groups rather than deciphering word by word

• acquiring sufficient speed to make fluent reading with comprehension possible

Certain classroom activities can help to further these objectives.

1. The instructor can periodically read aloud to the students, phrase by phrase, while they follow in their books and repeat each phrase immediately afterward, in chorus. The phrases may be short at first, and gradually grow longer. The instructor can encourage the students to continue reading in this manner, even when reading silently, by occasionally having one student read aloud.

2. Reading aloud will be more effective if the other students do not follow along in their books. While one student reads, the others should have their books *closed* and should try to grasp the meaning entirely from the reader's voice. Classes unused to this method find it challenging at first, but soon grow accustomed to it if the instructor perseveres. The instructor can also interrupt the reader from time to time to question the class on points of vocabulary, grammar, and meaning.

3. The instructor may prepare language laboratory tapes to supplement the readings. One method is to read an article phrase by phrase onto the tape, leaving a pause between each phrase so that the student can repeat what was said. A valuable variation on the repetition method is to have the student try to *anticipate* the instructor's phrasing on the second (and subsequent) passes through the tape. If the

student reads the phrase *before* the instructor does, the instructor's voice will serve as a confirmation. This method also trains the student to read in meaningful thought groups.

These are only a few of the many techniques that experienced instructors use to develop reading skills in an atmosphere of lively oral give-and-take. We would enjoy hearing from any users of this book who may want to tell us about teaching techniques that they are using successfully.

ENCOUNTERS
AN · ESL · READER

Third Edition

When the Cherry Blossoms Bloom

1

Maryen
Define wordis.

are . . . are open, in color
② ③opcions

participate . . . do things
with other people
No flowers

example

Pegulor vnbs
or Ivegulov venb's

April in Washington, D.C., is the time when the famous cherry trees are in full bloom.° Hundreds of thousands of visitors from all over the world come to admire the pink and white blossoms and to participate in° the week-long Cherry Blossom Festival.

The trees are a symbol° of long-lasting friendship and cooperation between the United States and Japan. In 1909 Helen Taft, the wife of the president, William Howard Taft, wanted to plant a few cherry trees in a new park near the Potomac River. Dr. Jokichi Takamine, a well-known Japanese scientist visiting the United States at that time, learned of Mrs. Taft's wish and arranged for the trees to be sent from Tokyo. But instead of a few trees, the capital city of Japan sent three thousand trees of twelve different varieties!

beside

They arrived in Seattle, Washington, in 1912 and went by train to the nation's capital. The first tree was planted by Mrs. Taft on March 27th of that year and the wife of the Japanese ambassador planted a second one alongside° the first. These trees are still standing today, among the thousands of others.

honors

yearly

lantern

The Cherry Blossom Festival commemorates° the planting of those first trees and has become an annual° event. Special concerts, plays, and displays of oriental art, music, and dance are available to the public free or for a small charge. The city's museums stay open late and the spring tour of the White House garden usually takes place that week.

The festival begins each year with a parade and the lighting of the Japanese stone lantern° that was a gift from the governor

Many of the visitors want
to tour the White House.

of Tokyo in 1954. The lantern is eight and one-half feet high, weighs six hundred pounds, and is three hundred years old. Another gift from Japan was the Mikimoto crown,° to be worn by the young woman chosen as Cherry Blossom queen. The crown is made of solid gold and has 1,585 pearls. Because it is so heavy, the queen wears the crown for only a short time and then changes it for a miniature° gold and pearl one which she can keep when the festival is over.

Even though the cherry blossoms bloom every year, no one can tell exactly on which day they will open and be at their most beautiful. This usually happens between April 5th and April 22nd, but the blossoms have come as early as March 20th and as late as May 1st. Since they only remain in full color for about a week, everyone hopes that they will bloom during the festival, and, luckily, that is almost always what happens.

[441 words]

crown

small

Adapted from National Cherry Blossom Publications

The lantern and cherry trees are symbols of the countries' friendship.

EXERCISES

Vocabulary

A   *Complete the sentence with a word or expression from the article.*

1. The city that is a country's center of government is called the
   ~~Capital~~ city.
2. When two things are next to one another, we say that one is
   ~~beside~~ the other.
3. We are not certain of the time the cherry blossoms will open. We
   do not know ~~Exactly~~ when this will happen.
4. When the cherry blossoms are open, we say they are in ~~Color~~.
5. The visitors can ~~Articipate~~ in the many things to do during the festival.
6. The Mikimoto crown is ~~Worn~~ by the Cherry Blossom queen.
7. The cherry trees help you to remember the friendship between
   Japan and the United States. They are ~~Examp~~ of that friendship.
8. Most of the events during the festival are ~~Available~~ without any
   charge.

B *Choose the most accurate of the three statements.*

1. The crown is made of solid gold.
    a) It is very heavy.
    b) It is made only of gold.
    c) It is made only of gold and pearls.
2. These two trees are still standing.
    a) The trees are in the same place they were planted.
    b) The trees are standing still.
    c) The trees are among thousands of others.
3. He learned of Mrs. Taft's wish.
    a) He sent her the cherry trees.
    b) He found out what she wanted.
    c) He wished her to learn about the cherry trees.
4. Instead of a few trees, they sent three thousand trees of twelve different varieties.
    a) Instead of the trees, they sent twelve different varieties.
    b) They sent three thousand, instead of twelve, varieties.
    c) They sent many more trees than were expected.
5. No one can tell when the blossoms will open.
    a) No one tells you when the blossoms will open.
    b) You can't tell anyone when the blossoms will open.
    c) No one knows when the blossoms will open.
6. They only remain in full color for about a week.
    a) They are most beautiful for about a week.
    b) They are fully open for about a week.
    c) Only the blossoms remain in full color for about a week.
7. She can keep the crown when the festival is over.
    a) She can wear the crown over the festival.
    b) She does not have to give back the crown after the festival.
    c) She can keep the crown if she wears it during the festival.
8. She planted a second tree alongside the first.
    a) Besides the first tree, she planted a second one.
    b) First she planted one tree; then she planted a second tree.
    c) Next to the first tree, she planted a second one.

Correct the sentence if it is false according to the article. **True or False**

1. The trees may bloom on April 1st. F The Trees May bloom between April 5ht and April 22nd.
2. The lantern is planted alongside the second tree. F The lantern was a Gift of the Governor
3. Dr. Takamine was the Japanese ambassador in 1909. F Dr Takamine was a Japanes Scientist
4. Today, no one remembers where the first two trees were planted. F They were Planted Near the Potouiac River
5. Miniature crowns are given to the visitors. F The Miniature crown is Given To the Queen
6. The visitors must stay in Washington for a full week. T

The Washington
Monument stands tall
behind blossoming
cherry trees.

the lantern was another gift from Japan

7. The crown, but not the lantern, was a gift from Japan. F

8. Mrs. Taft wanted to plant three thousand cherry trees in
   Washington. F *Mrs. Taft wanted to plant a few Cherry Trees*

Questions

1. Why do the Cherry Blossom queens wear miniature crowns?
2. Why didn't the ambassador's wife plant the second tree in 1909?
3. In what part of Washington are the cherry trees planted?
4. Why do so many visitors come to Washington in April?
5. Who was president of the United States in 1912?
6. What can visitors to Washington do during the Cherry Blossom
   Festival?
7. In what way are Tokyo and Washington alike?
8. What was different about the 1954 festival?

Structures

A Many people visit Washington. *→they would*
   If many people visited Washington, they'd all be happier.

1. Thousands of visitors return each year.
2. They remember the beauty of the trees.

3. They know the color of the blossoms.
4. The young women wear the crown.
5. The visitors go to many shows.
6. All the citizens cooperate with each other.
7. The tourists become interested in seeing the city.
8. They remain in the sun for about a week.

B   He's an ambassador.   →   **He's not an ambassador, is he?**
       That's a cherry tree.   →   **That's not a cherry tree, is it?**

1. She's the Cherry Blossom queen. *She's not the Cherry Blossom Queen, is she?*
2. That's the capital city. *that's not te capital city, is it?*
3. Those are symbols of friendship. *Those aren't symbols of Friendship, are those?*
4. They're returning to Washington. *They're not returning To washington, Are they?*
5. It's sending all the trees. *It's not sending all the trees,*
6. This is the miniature crown. *This is not the miniature crown, is it?*
7. We're cooperating. *we're not cooperating, are we?*
8. They're the ones who come back every year. *They're not the ones who come back every year, are they?*

C   STUDENT 1: Will *all the visitors* return *to Washington?*   →
       STUDENT 2: **No, I guess some won't return there.**
       STUDENT 1: Will *all the people* remember *the festival?*   →
       STUDENT 2: **No, I guess some won't remember it.**

1. Will *all the trees* stand *in the park?*
2. Will *all the blossoms* open *during the festival?*
3. Will *all the ambassadors* plant *the trees?*
4. Will *all the queens* wear *the miniature crown?*
5. Will *all the displays* be free *all week?*
6. Will *all the blossoms* bloom *soon?*
7. Will *all the pearls* fit *on the crown?*
8. Will *all of our class* meet *the ambassador's wife?*

Number the events in the order in which they occurred according to the story.   **Sequencing**

1. _____ Hundreds of thousands of people visit Washington.
2. _____ Dr. Takamine made the arrangements.
3. _____ The ambassador's wife planted a tree.
4. _____ Mrs. Taft wanted to plant some trees.
5. _____ The stone lantern was presented to begin the festival.
6. _____ Mrs. Taft planted a tree.
7. _____ Tokyo sent three thousand cherry trees.
8. _____ William Howard Taft became president of the United States.

Word Families

short → **shortly**

1.	week	5.	usual
2.	different	6.	solid
3.	annual	7.	lucky
4.	beautiful	8.	exact

Points of View

1. "Governments have more important things to do than spend time and money sending trees to one another." Do you agree or disagree? Why?

2. Some people think that choosing a pretty, young woman as a "queen," and giving her a crown to wear, is really foolish and insulting to all women, and that all of these "beauty contests" should be stopped. Do you think this is a good idea? Why or why not?

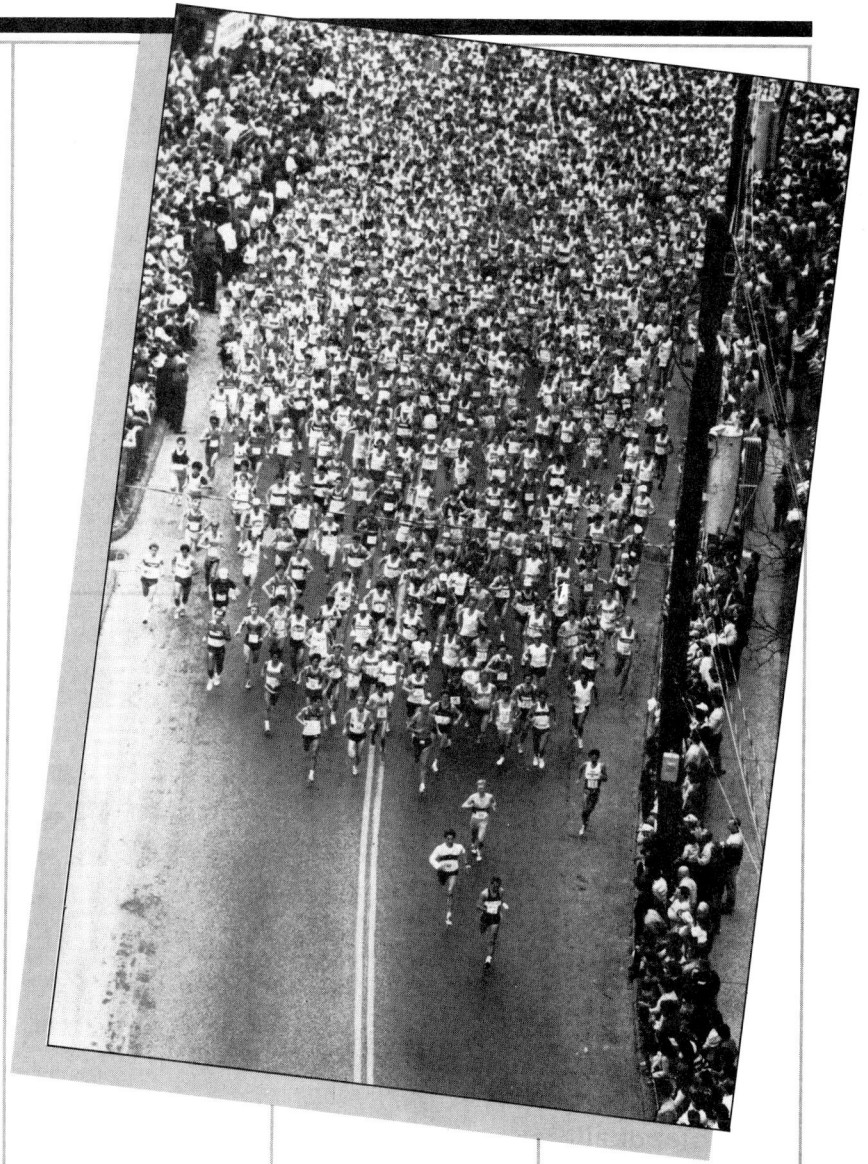

2
Everybody's Jogging

bench

As the young woman ran by, the old man sitting on the park bench° asked, "What are you running for?" The woman smiled. "I'm not running, I'm jogging," she said, and she continued her slow run through the park.

Every day, in all kinds of weather, many thousands of men and women jog. Why has jogging—running slowly for long distances—become so popular? Most joggers begin because they hear it is very good exercise. Jogging makes the heart stronger and helps people lose weight. It can also help them feel better about themselves.

Donald Robbins, who is forty-two years old and works in an office, began jogging a few years ago because he felt he was too fat. At first he could only run about one hundred yards. It took him three months to be able to run a mile. But two years later, he ran in a marathon race—over twenty-six miles. Many joggers, like Donald Robbins, feel that if they can succeed at jogging

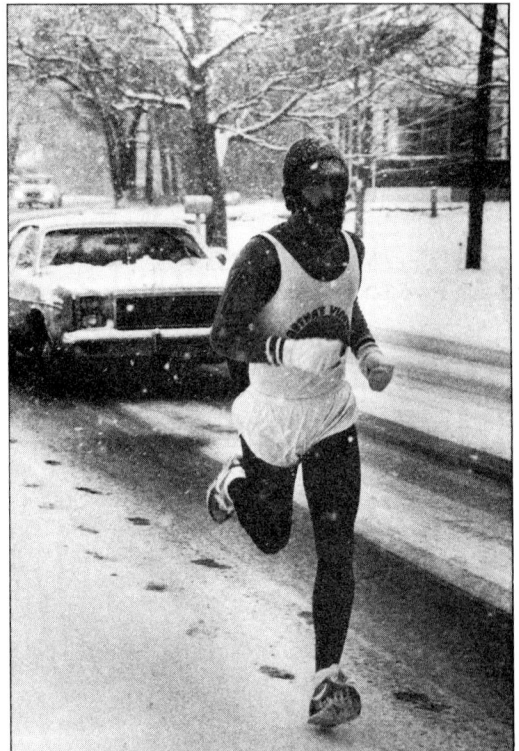

Joggers are out
in all kinds of weather.

A good pair of shoes is the only special clothing needed.

they can succeed at other things also, and quite often this feeling helps them at their jobs.°

the work a person does

Should you jog too? If you want to jog, be sure to ask your doctor for advice first. Jogging may be too much exercise for you.

Does jogging cost much? No, it costs almost nothing. But it is very important to have a good pair of shoes that were made especially for jogging. They protect your feet and legs from the shock of running on hard surfaces.

How fast should you go? Jog with a friend and talk to each other as you run. If you have difficulty talking, you're going too fast.

How far should you jog? Remember not to go too far too soon. In fact, you should walk, not run, the first few times. Then do some short jogs, but no more than what you can do comfortably. After that, increase your distance a quarter or half mile every two weeks or so. Maybe in a few years you too can run in a marathon. Thousands of people do.

[345 words]

Adapted from Nation's Business

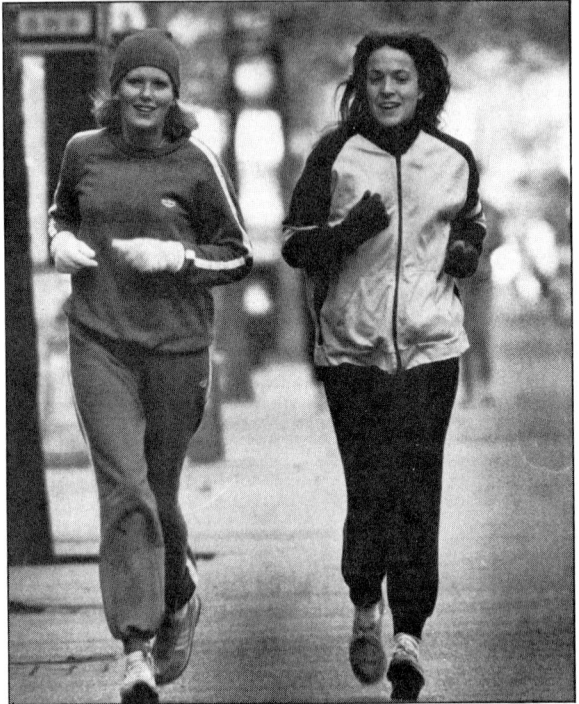

Take a friend with
you when you jog.

Gramar book.
Chapter One
For next Wednsday.

EXERCISES

Next
For wednesday

Vocabulary

A *Complete the sentence with a word or expression from the article.*

1. Many people jog. Jogging has become very popular.
2. Some people are not sure that jogging would be good for them. They should ask a doctor for advice.
3. You shouldn't jog in your regular shoes. Wear shoes that are made specially for jogging.
4. A marathon race is over twenty-six miles long.
5. If you can do well at jogging, you may succeed at your job also.
6. Start by running only a quarter mile, and then increase your distance a little each week.
7. Don't do too much at first. Only run as far as you can go comfortably before you try to do more.
8. You should be able to run easily, and not find it too hard to talk while running.

B *Choose the most accurate of the three statements.*

1. A person smiles with his or her
   a) feet and legs.
   b) special clothing.
   c) mouth and face.
2. To continue is to
   a) keep on doing something.
   b) run with a friend.
   c) go only a little way.
3. They increased the distance.
   a) They ran faster.
   b) They ran only a little way at first.
   c) They ran further.
4. He was successful at his job.
   a) He did his work well.
   b) He began his work slowly.
   c) He was not too tired at work.
5. Robbins asked his doctor for advice.
   a) He wanted to be successful at work.
   b) He wasn't sure it was good for him.
   c) He ran only a little way at first.
6. Don't go too far too soon.
   a) Go only a little way at first.
   b) Walk the first few times.
   c) Talk while going the distance.
7. He felt he was too fat.
   a) He knew it.
   b) He had doubts.
   c) He thought so.
8. They jogged by the park bench.
   a) at it
   b) past it
   c) toward it

have to
"Use Dictionary"
Understand Part's of Speech

C *Fill in the blanks with the noun suggested by the verb in italics.*
Then read the sentences aloud.

1. He *feels* good; he has a good Feeling.
2. He *succeeded* at running; he was a success at running.
3. I will *continue* to exercise; continuity of the exercise will help me.
4. The race *began* slowly; the beginning of the race was slow.
5. You were *racing* with your friend; you had a race with her.
6. The doctor *lost* weight; he had a weight loss
7. They *started* to run slowly; their start was slow.
8. My shoes *cost* twenty dollars; their cost is high.

The nouns only.

happy: adj, n.
noun.
happyness
adverb.
happily

the Verb maybe loxe /ce the noun.
lose V → loss related
loose Adjetive

Structures

A   She wears special shoes. →
Does she wear special shoes?

1. He comes running by. *Does He come runnmy by?*
2. It takes him three months. *Does it take three months?*
3. They run for exercise. *Do they run For exercise?*
4. He starts out slowly. *Does He Start out Slow!Y him?*
5. His friend jogs with him. *Is his Friend Jog whit him?*
6. She smiles at the old man. *Does she smile at the old men?*
7. He increases his distance each week. *Does he increase his distance each week?*
8. Robbins feels he can succeed at jogging. *Does Robbins Feel he can succeed at Jogging?*

B   How fast is he talking? →
He isn't talking too fast. He's not talking too fast.

1. How far is she going? *She isn't going too Far.*
2. How much is he spending? *He isn't spending too much.*
3. How many races is he running? *He is not running too many races.*
4. How hard is she exercising? *He is not exercising too hard.*
5. How well is she succeeding? *She isn't succeedin very well.*
6. How comfortable are they feeling? *They aren't Feeling too conFort able.*
7. How slowly is she running? *She isn't running too slowly*
8. How fast is the doctor working? *He is not working too Fast.*

C   Perhaps he can run a mile. →
He may be able to run a mile.

1. Perhaps he can jog next week. *He may be able to jog next week*
2. Perhaps her friend can talk to her. *Her Friend may be able to talk To Her*
3. Perhaps the doctor can tell him. *The Doctor may be able to tell him*
4. Perhaps the old man can exercise. *The old men may be able to do Exercise*
5. Perhaps we can lose weight. *We may be able to lose weight*
6. Perhaps the banker can run in the park. *The banker may be able To run in the Park*
7. Perhaps you can jog with my friend. *You may be able To jog whith my Friend.*
8. Perhaps I can buy special clothing. *I may be able to buy special clothiny.*

True or False

Correct the sentence if it is false according to the article.

1. If you wear special shoes, you can jog faster. *F*
2. Donald Robbins is a successful doctor. *F*
3. Joggers should run slower at night than during the day. *F*
4. If you are fat, you should begin by walking, not jogging. *T*
5. If you are not fat, you should begin by walking, not jogging. *T*
6. Jogging shoes protect your feet. *T*

7. It takes longer to run a marathon than it does to jog three miles.
8. You must wait two years before you can run in a marathon. *F*

Questions

1. Why does Donald Robbins feel good about himself?
2. Why is it good to talk while jogging?
3. Which people should see a doctor before they begin jogging?
4. How long is a marathon race?
5. What is the difference between jogging and running?
6. How can jogging help you at your job?
7. Why do you think some people jog at night?
8. Why do so many people jog?

Points of View

1. If jogging is so healthful, why doesn't everybody jog?
2. What is your favorite kind of exercise? What are its advantages and disadvantages?
3. What else should people do to stay healthy?

A Woman in the Window

3

She leads a short life, but a very rich one. She wears many beautiful and expensive dresses, marvelous furs and jewels, and she is seen in the best stores. She has people to dress her and keep her face pretty. Still, even though she has thousands of admirers, she rarely smiles. Although she is beautiful, she rarely meets men of her own kind. She gets all dressed up, it seems, just to impress other women. She is, as you might have guessed, the mannequin who gazes° dreamily from store windows.

    Some of the people who design window displays° think of mannequins only as objects to work with, but most of the people who make use of the figures call them by name. Although a mannequin has a number given to it by the manufacturer,° it is very often known by the name of the woman who modeled for it. And, like a living model, "she" is chosen because her appearance goes well with the styles of a particular clothing de-

looks

design . . . plan what they look like

company that makes something

Mannequins get all dressed up in expensive furs and clothing.

Some people who design store windows think of mannequins as objects.

signer. "You never say, 'Bring me number twelve,'" explains Bob Filoso of the Wolf and Vine mannequin company. "You say, 'Get Sally, or Rosa.'"

What the stores look for these days are <u>interesting</u>, rather than perfect, faces. Like Sara Kapp's, for example. She is a professional model° whose look-alike, produced by the Adel Root-stein company, has been very popular. Sara's long nose and green eyes make her face unusual rather than beautiful.

As fashions change, not only are there changes in faces, but changes in pose.° The figures have become more realistic. Until a few years ago, mannequins were made without toes. But now that open shoes have become popular, toes are necessary. "When pants were very popular, mannequins stood differently," says Candy Pratts, who directs window designers at Bloomingdale's, a large New York store. "Now they stand in a more relaxed° way, better for dresses."

Even though a mannequin gets excellent care, her life in a good store is not likely to be more than two years. Bloomingdale's has 160 manniquins in use, and Candy Pratts says her department buys some new ones every two months. And that,

professional . . . one who makes a living from modeling

the way a person stands

not stiff

Sara Kapp's look-alike
has been very popular.

Now they stand in a more relaxed way, better for dresses.

she adds, is why it's best not to get used to any particular mannequin. "When I get a favorite, I hate to see her go."

[379 words]

Adapted from *The New York Times*

EXERCISES

Vocabulary

A   *Supply the missing words.*

1. If something is Expensive it costs a lot of money.
2. A mannequin should look beautiful, so that people can imagine them-
    selves wearing the clothes.
3. The mannequin had the same face as Sara Kapp. She was Sara's
    model
4. One part of a store sells shoes; another Department sells dresses.
5. The people who make mannequins give them numbers instead
    of names.

6. Mannequins are _likely_ used for more than two years.

[handwritten: ProbAblemeinte]

7. To show mannequins in store windows is to _____ them. *[handwritten: sell cloth for]*

8. Designers who use numbers for mannequins just think of them as _objects_ to use in windows.

B *Choose the most accurate of the three statements.*

1. She had a perfect face.
   a) She was beautiful.
   b) She had a long nose and green eyes.
   c) She looked very realistic.

2. A favorite mannequin is one that is
   a) liked more than others.
   b) less than two years old.
   c) in a relaxed pose.

3. To impress other women is to
   a) have an effect on their feelings.
   b) show them how to get dressed.
   c) gaze at them from store windows.

4. One kind of manufacturer is a
   a) professional model.
   b) mannequin maker.
   c) design director.

5. Someone who is popular is
   a) relaxed.
   b) a professional model.
   c) liked by many people.

6. Today's fashions are
   a) more realistic.
   b) those worn now.
   c) beautiful and expensive.

7. One who leads an expensive life
   a) is changed every two years.
   b) wears furs and jewels.
   c) has a number first, then a name.

8. A particular mannequin is
   a) any one.
   b) that one.
   c) no one.

C *Supply the missing words.*

1. A _model_ makes a living posing for photos.
2. A _mannequin Designer_ arranges models in store windows; a _designer_ creates the things the models wear.
3. A person who is looking at nothing in particular is _a mannequin._

4. One model stands one way; another stands another way—their _poses_ are different.
5. A perfect face may not be as _beautiful_ as one that is a little unusual.
6. Mannequins that are more _relaxed_ look better in dresses.
7. Toes are _necessary_ when mannequins wear open shoes.
8. Since they are expensive, mannequins get _excellent_ care.

singe

Structures

A   She is a mannequin. She gazes dreamily from store windows.   →
She is the mannequin who gazes dreamily from store windows.

1. Wolf and Vine is a company. Wolf and Vine manufactures mannequins.
2. Sara Kapp is a model. Sara Kapp is currently popular.
3. Bloomingdale's is a large store. Bloomingdale's has beautiful clothing.
4. Candy Pratts is a designer. Candy Pratts uses only certain mannequins.
5. That woman is a shopper. That woman wears expensive clothes.
6. He is a male model. He is not used very often.
7. They are manufacturers. They call mannequins by name.
8. They are expensive clothes. They are not seen very often.

B   She won't last more than two years.   →
She is not likely to last more than two years.

1. I won't go to that store again.
2. Sally won't meet her admirers there.
3. They won't call her by name any more.
4. The store won't buy any more mannequins this month.
5. The shape of the body won't change.
6. Mannequin makers won't use beautiful models.
7. Her personality won't go well with the clothes of that designer.
8. They won't use male mannequins very often.

C   She liked that mannequin.   →
She got used to liking that mannequin.

1. She tried on the clothes.
2. Candy called for that model.
3. Bob changed the window.
4. Sara looked at her look-alike.
5. Wolf and Vine made the design.
6. She bought the dresses.
7. The designer worked with the new mannequins.
8. He used that face.

Correct the statement if it is false according to the article. **True or False**

1. Candy Pratts directs window designers at a large store.
2. Bloomingdale's uses 160 new mannequins every two months.
3. Mannequins are often known by the names of real people.
4. A relaxed pose is best for displaying pants.
5. Pants look better on certain mannequins than they do on others.
6. A mannequin wears the same clothing for two years.
7. A model can be beautiful even though her face is not perfect.
8. Manufacturers change the shape and pose of their mannequins every two years.

Questions

1. Why do mannequins have a short life?
2. Why are mannequins given names instead of numbers?
3. Where are mannequins usually found when they are "working"?
4. Why are mannequins made in different poses?
5. Why doesn't an old mannequin have toes?
6. What kinds of faces do stores look for?
7. About how often are mannequins changed?
8. Why are certain mannequins chosen for certain clothes?

Points of View

1. How do you think Sara Kapp feels when she sees her face in so many store windows? How do you think she will feel in two years?
2. What kind of woman would you rather meet (or be)—one with an interesting face or one with a perfect face? Why?

Discussion

"It's such a waste to use mannequins for only two years." What do you think of this statement? What other ways can you think of to use mannequins?

They No Longer Move: Mobile Homes

4

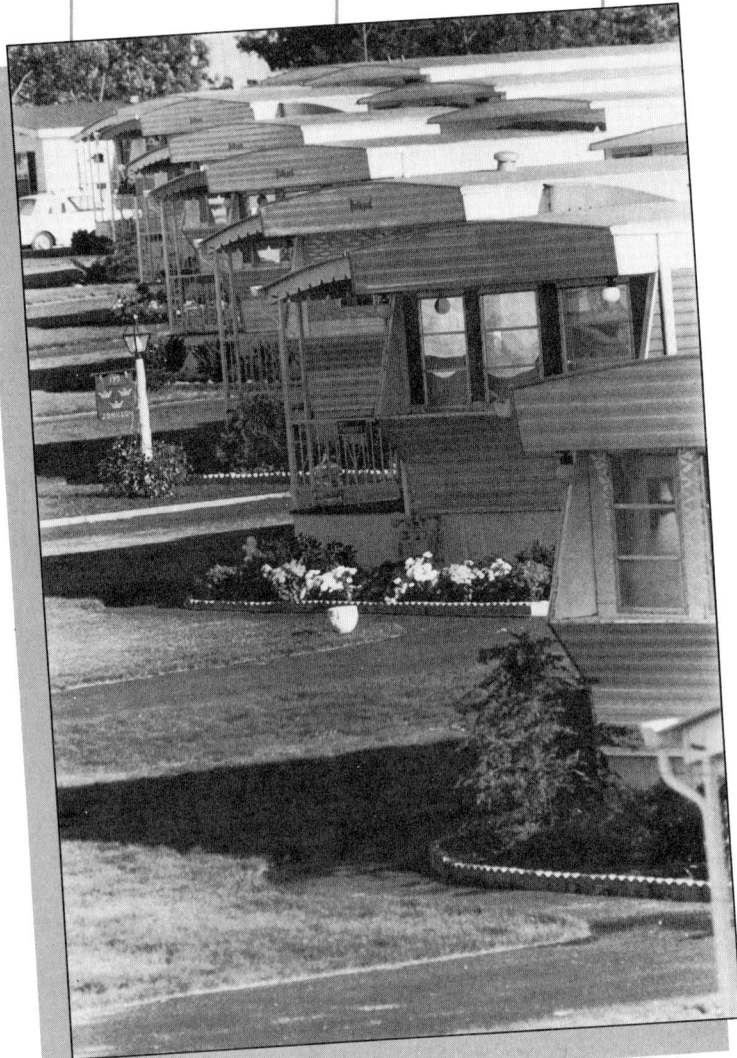

The dictionary says that "mobile" means "capable of being° easily and quickly moved." Yet to more and more Americans, the words "mobile home" mean something very different—a new and settled way of life.

capable... able to be

"We were tired of paying rent on a small apartment, and we didn't have enough money to buy a house, but we still wanted something that was our own," Jackie Brighton explained while she fed her young child. "Now we have land and room for a garden. We're certain that we'll be here for a number of years."

The freedom to move from one part of the United States to another has always been part of the country's traditions.° But in the last ten or fifteen years, this movement, or mobility, has slowed down. Families still move, mostly to the Sunbelt—the southern and western parts of the country, where the weather is usually warmer. But the number of people who move from place to place is smaller than it used to be.

customs that have been followed for many years

ity = NOUN
Florida, Arizona, California

POST

Many of the people who decide to stay in one location are finding new homes, places that look mobile though they really are not. Years ago, they were called trailers,° and were pulled

trailer

Residents may decorate their yards as they please.

behind cars or trucks. They offered complete accommodations°
for eating and sleeping; at night the families could stop driving
and move into them.

Now, many of these trailers don't move at all, and families
live in them just as they would in regular houses. Thousands of
mobile home "parks" have been established all over the country
for this growing number of new residents.° The homes are made
more permanent° by attaching° them to electricity and water
supplies. The owners decorate° them just as they would a house
in any other neighborhood. Many families, like the Brightons,
have even planted flower and vegetable gardens around their
mobile homes, making them completely nonmobile.

Older couples, retired° from their jobs, seem to like mobile
home living as much as younger couples do. Many of the parks
are especially for these senior citizens. No children are allowed,
noise is kept down,° and the parks have special activities that
older people can enjoy.

Ed and Marcella Powers had often visited her mother, who
had retired to a mobile home park. They thought it was such a
convenient° way to live that, when they sold their house, they
didn't hesitate° to move their furniture into a new three-bedroom
mobile home. Their sixteen-year-old daughter Denise has her

spaces

*people who live, or "reside,"
in a place*

*not movable / joining or
connecting*

make them look nice

not working anymore

kept . . . kept at a low level

easy

wait long

The school bus stops at
the front gate.

own room. She gets on the school bus at the park's front gate, and even her dog, Pito, seems to enjoy the life.

Mr. and Mrs. Powers are only twenty minutes away from their jobs. But what they like most is the <u>friendliness</u> in the trailer park. "When we lived in a house, we only knew the family next door," Mrs. Powers says. "Here, we never come home from work without blowing the horn° or waving to three or four people on the street. It's really home for us."

Negative
Simple Present

blowing the horn

There is one problem: because the mobile homes are lighter than regular houses and are not firmly attached to foundations, they can be damaged by heavy <u>storms</u> and <u>high winds</u>. The people who live in them, however, are prepared to take this <u>risk</u>.° They say that the pleasure of the life is worth it.

possibility of danger

How America Will Change in the Coming Years

How - where.

The Census Bureau is the government department that, every decade,° counts the number of people living in the United States, and also puts together a great deal of information about how and where Americans live and work. From this information, the Census Bureau has some ideas about the changes that will take place in American <u>living and working patterns</u>° in the years ahead.

ten years

the way people do things

Adjetive

- Twenty years <u>ago, many</u> people were moving from the "country"—<u>farms and small towns</u>—to larger cities, but this seems to have stopped. In fact, there were more people living in the "country" in 1980 than there were in 1960.

- More and more people of all ages are living in the Sunbelt. This area—the warmer southern and western parts of the country—had a population increase of almost 45% between <u>1970 and 1980</u>, while the north, east, and central parts grew less than 5%. <u>Even so, the number of people who have moved from place to place is smaller than it used to be.</u>

- Population growth is <u>slowing down.</u> Between 1950 and 1960, the country's population increased by 18.5%. From 1960 to 1970 the growth was down to 13.4% and between

Progressive Sentence

Special activities are available at many of the parks.

1970 and 1980 the number of people grew only 11.4%.

- Children are staying in school longer. Most people have finished twelve years or more in school.
- People are getting married later. In 1980, most men getting married for the first time were about twenty-five years of age.
- There are more working women. In 1980, over 50% of all the women in the U.S. were working. In 1960, this number was only 37.8%.

[837 words]

Adapted from *The Christian Science Monitor* and *U.S. News & World Report*

EXERCISES

Vocabulary ✗ A *Supply the missing words.*

1. The number of people who move is smaller than it used to be.
2. The owners decorate their homes with flowers and vegetable gardens.

decorate

especially

3. Many of the parks are _especially_ for senior citizens.
4. Her mother _retired_ to a mobile home park. *retired*
5. We always _blow_ the horn on our car when we come home.
6. Families live in mobile homes just as they would in _regular_ houses. —*regular*
7. A large _number_ of people move from place to place every year. — *number*
8. One of the country's _tradition_ is the freedom to move. —*tradition* *Wendsday.*
Tradition.

★ **B** *Which of the following sentences or phrases has the same meaning*
as the model?

1. Families still move.
   a) Families continue to move.
   b) Families are still.
   c) Moving families are still.
   d) Even families move.
2. on the other hand
   a) either left or right
   b) the other way
   c) however
   d) handily
3. nowadays
   a) these days
   b) today
   c) any time today
   d) during the day
4. We never come home without waving to our friends.
   a) We never wave until we come home.
   b) We always wave to our friends.
   c) When we don't come home, we don't wave.
   d) We wave to our friends from our car.
5. Noise is kept down.
   a) The noise is kept below the mobile home parks.
   b) The noise is kept in the mobile homes.
   c) No noise is allowed.
   d) Not much noise is allowed. —*permitido*
6. They are only twenty minutes from their jobs.
   a) They are not far from home.
   b) They work near their home. ★
   c) They work in their home.
   d) They work near their jobs.
7. It's really home for us.
   a) We like it here. ★
   b) We left our home.
   c) We planted flowers around our home.
   d) We know the family in the next house.

8. They didn't hesitate to move their furniture.
   a) They didn't wait to move their furniture.
   b) They only moved their furniture.
   c) They moved quickly.
   d) They didn't move quickly.

True or False

Correct the sentence if it is false according to the article.

F 1. Many senior citizens move into their trailers at night.
T 2. Not as many people are moving from place to place anymore.
T 3. More women than men are working.
   4. Planting flowers near a mobile home helps to make it nonmobile.
T 5. People who live in mobile homes often move them to the Sunbelt.
F 6. The eastern part of the country has stopped growing.
F 7. Most people about twelve years old have finished school.
F 8. People have to sell their old furniture when they move into a mobile home.

Questions

1. What is a mobile home park?
2. Why do many senior citizens like to live in mobile home parks?
3. What is the difference between a trailer and a mobile home?
4. Where do more people live—in cities or in the country?
5. Why do people decorate their mobile homes?
6. Why does the Census Bureau say that population growth is slowing down?
7. What did Mr. and Mrs. Powers do with their furniture when they moved to a mobile home?
8. In 1980, how old were most men when they first got married?

Structures

A They are happy in the mobile home park. →
   Are they really happy in the mobile home park?

1. Mobile homes are good places for senior citizens to live.
2. People are getting married later.
3. Population growth is slowing down.
4. The Census Bureau is the department that counts the people.
5. Mobile homes are pulled behind cars or trucks.
6. Movement to the Sunbelt is slowing down.
7. There are more working women now.
8. The homes are made permanent by attaching them to water supplies.

B The number of people grows *11.4% each year.* →
How much does the number of people grow?

1. Most families move *to the Sunbelt.*
2. They like mobile home life *because it is friendly.*
3. We plant *vegetable gardens* around our home.
4. *Many senior citizens* live in mobile home parks.
5. The Census Bureau puts together a *great deal of information.*
6. Population growth is *slowing down.*
7. More women are *working.*
8. Most men get married *at about twenty-five years of age.*

C They are decorating their homes nicely. →
They are trying their best to decorate their homes nicely.

1. We are pulling our trailer behind our car.
2. He is keeping warm in the Sunbelt.
3. They are saving their money to buy a house.
4. Children are staying in school longer.
5. I am attaching it to the water supply.
6. We are selling our old home.
7. She is feeding her four-month-old child.
8. Mr. Brighton is keeping the noise down.

D I like it here. →
Mr. Brighton likes it here. Mr. and Mrs. Brighton like it here. The Brighton family likes it here.

1. I am tired of paying rent on a small apartment.
2. I wave from the car when I come home.
3. I go to Florida every year.
4. I keep the noise down.
5. I stop driving at night.
6. I keep moving from place to place.
7. I do not enjoy cold weather.
8. I have a flower garden.

E Where do they like to live? In the Sunbelt? →
Yes, they do like to live in the Sunbelt.

1. What do they call them? Mobile home parks?
2. Who does she wave to? Her neighbors?
3. Where does she get on the bus? At the front gate?

4. What does the Census Bureau count? The number of people?
5. What do the children do? Make noise?
6. When do they leave for work? At 8 A.M.?
7. Who does she visit? Her mother?
8. How do you live in a mobile home? Just as you would in a regular house?

Imagination

1. *(for two students at a time)*
   Pretend you visited a mobile home park yesterday. One of you liked it and one didn't. Talk to each other for three minutes about the experience. What was it like? Describe the homes. Who did you see there? What were they doing? Why would you (or wouldn't you) like to live there?
2. Pretend you and your family live in a mobile home and are happy with that kind of life. Then pretend you have just learned that sometimes there are dangerous storms in your area and that your home could be damaged by them. Would you be "prepared to take this risk"? Why or why not?

5

Herrero

The City
Blacksmith

cerrajero

The police still use
horses in New York.

horseshoe

hoof

New York is one of the last large American cities to have some
of its police officers on horseback. The New York police have
170 horses that they use in certain parts of the city. The horses
are expensive to feed, but it is even more expensive to take care
of them in other ways. Because the horses must walk on the
streets, they need special horseshoes.° In fact, they need more
than eight thousand of them each year. Every police horse in
New York gets new shoes every month. Keeping these shoes in
good repair is the job of six blacksmiths. There are only about
thirty-five of these blacksmiths in the whole United States.

Shoeing a horse costs between twenty and thirty-five dollars,
and it takes a skilled blacksmith two to three hours to do the
job.

A blacksmith's job is not an easy one. He must be able to
shape a shoe from a piece of plain metal and then fit it to the
horse's hoof.° The blacksmith must bend over all the time he is

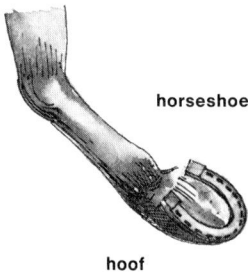

fitting the shoe and must hold the weight of the horse's leg while he works. Clearly, a blacksmith must be very strong. But even more important, he must be able to deal with° horses—for before the blacksmith can begin his work, he has to get the horse to lift its leg.

deal . . . get them to do what he wants

One of the blacksmiths in New York is James Corbin, who came to this country from Ireland in 1948. He not only shoes horses for the police, but also works for a racetrack° and for a group of horseowners who live near the city. Corbin became interested in blacksmithing because his father did it, and, as he puts it, "It's a good way to make a living."°

Vino

Hipodromo

place where horses race

good . . . a nice job

[291 words]

Adapted from *Sports Illustrated*

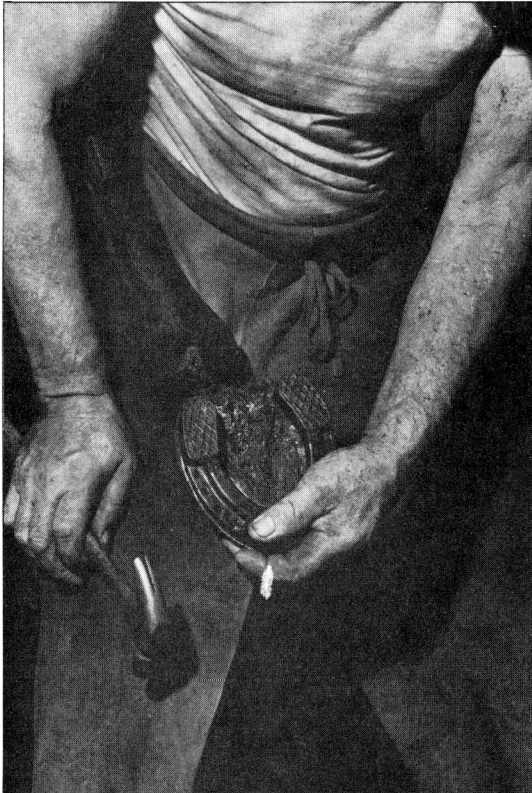

Horses that walk on streets need special horseshoes.

EXERCISES

[handwritten: Quiz]

Identification

Complete the following statements about the picture below.

1. The blacksmith is ~~fitting~~ the horse.
2. In order to shoe the horse, the blacksmith has to *[handwritten: bend]* over.
3. The blacksmith has gotten the horse to *[handwritten: lift]* its leg.
4. *[handwritten: ✗]* The blacksmith is trying to *[handwritten: shape]* the shoe to the horse's *[handwritten: hoof]*.
5. Identify as many parts of the man's body as possible: head, arm, and so forth.

Word Families

fit → **fitting** *[handwritten: Present Participle]*

[handwritten: (s or es) Rewrite the Plural]

horse → **horses**

1. repair *[handwritten: repairing]*
2. ride *[handwritten: riding]*
3. fix *[handwritten: Fixing]*
4. lift *[handwritten: lifting]*
5. shape *[handwritten: shaping]*
6. deal *[handwritten: dealing]*
7. get *[handwritten: getting]*
8. begin *[handwritten: beginning]*

1. shoe *[handwritten: shoes]*
2. blacksmith *[handwritten: blacksmiths]*
3. job *[handwritten: Jobs]*
4. horseshoe *[handwritten: hoseshoes]*
5. piece *[handwritten: Pieces]*
6. city *[handwritten: cities]*
7. policeman *[handwritten: Policemen]*
8. skill *[handwritten: skills]*

[handwritten: City Cities]

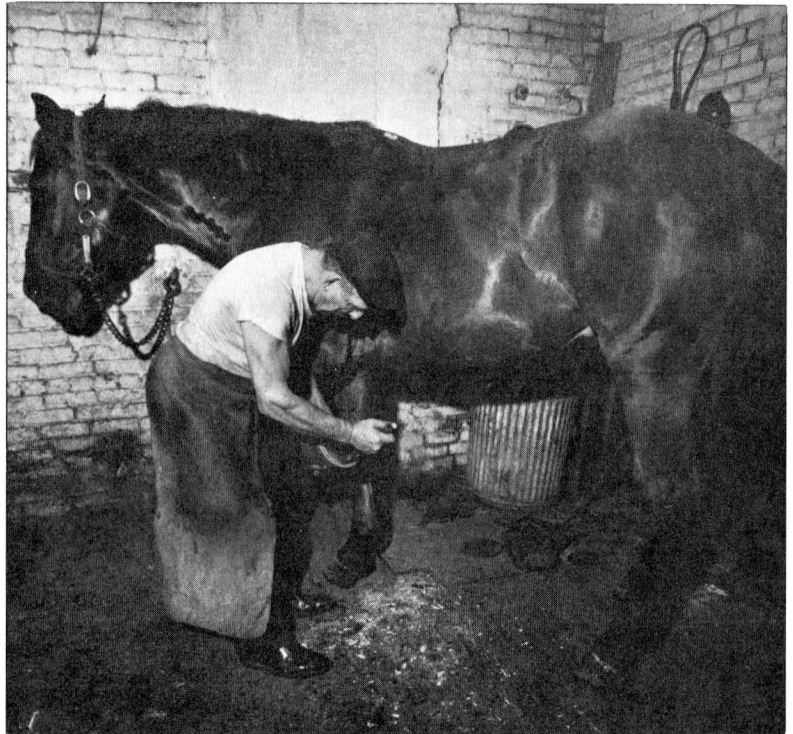

The blacksmith must hold the weight of the horse's leg while he works.

reading the history and understand it.

Choose the most accurate of the three statements. ✳

1. When police officers are on horseback, they are
   a) sitting on the horse.
   b) sitting in back of the horse.
   c) standing in back of the blacksmith.

To Monday

2. A horseshoe in good repair is one that is
   a) carried by a police officer.
   b) being fitted by a blacksmith.
   c) usable.
3. The man is very strong.
   a) He must be a blacksmith.
   b) He can work very hard.
   c) He deals with horses.
4. A skilled blacksmith *hábil tlewrena*
   a) is stronger than an unskilled blacksmith.
   b) knows how to deal with horses.
   c) can hold up a horse. *en cajón en la Pezuña*
5. The shoes do not fit the hoof.
   a) They cannot hold the horse's weight.
   b) They were made in three hours.
   c) They should be repaired.
6. The police need eight thousand horseshoes because
   a) there are only thirty-five blacksmiths.
   b) horse's legs are so heavy.
   c) the horses walk on the streets.
7. To shape a shoe is to
   a) fit it on the horse's foot.
   b) use it for two to three hours.
   c) bend a piece of metal.
8. A police horse is
   a) found only in New York.
   b) ridden by police officers. *moutado* ✳
   c) used at a racetrack.

A   He must get the horse to lift its leg.   →
   He has to get the horse to lift its leg.

1. He must shape the shoe.
2. They must repair the shoes.
3. Every horse must get new shoes.
4. The shoes must fit.
5. The city must use horses.
6. A blacksmith must have great strength.

7. A blacksmith must bend over while fitting the shoes.
8. The police officer must sit quietly on the horse.

B   Blacksmiths repair horseshoes.   →
     A blacksmith's job is to repair horseshoes.

1. Police officers protect people.
2. Teachers help people learn.
3. Racehorses run.
4. James Corbin shoes horses.
5. Students study.
6. Doctors give people advice.
7. Streetcleaners keep the streets clean.
8. Taxi drivers take people places.

True or False

Correct the sentence if it is false according to the article.

1. There are 170 city blacksmiths in the country.
2. If a horse got new shoes in October, it will not get new shoes again before December.
3. It takes two to three hours to get a horse to lift its leg.
4. There are many cities that have police officers on horseback.
5. A blacksmith bends over while he does his job.
6. Police officers change the horses' shoes every month.
7. Each horse gets its own special shoes.
8. A blacksmith must be able to deal with the police.

Questions

1. What kind of work does a blacksmith do?
2. How often does a police horse get new shoes?
3. How much does it cost to shoe a horse?
4. How long does it take to shoe a horse?
5. How many horses do the New York police have?
6. What does the blacksmith do with the horse's leg while he is fitting the shoe?
7. What must the blacksmith do before he can begin his work?
8. Why is a blacksmith's work hard?

Discussion

If you were a police officer, would you want to ride a horse? What can a police officer on horseback do that other police officers cannot? What would happen if there were no more city blacksmiths?

6

march
7
05/

Nancy Lopez

Sports have been an important part of American life for many years, first as something to watch and, increasingly, as something to do. American women have taken part in sports for a long time, but it is only in the last few years that they have come to be <u>recognized</u> as major athletes.° One of the <u>best known</u> of these is Nancy Lopez, who became a champion° golfer in 1978—when she was only twenty-one years old.

people who work hard at
sports
one who wins

Some people say that Nancy Lopez smiles even when she loses. Other people say that they are not so sure about that; they always see her smiling, but they haven't seen her lose. A large part of her popularity may be due to the fact that she always seems to be happy. Certainly some of it is due to the fact that she wins so often.

Nancy Lopez grew up in Roswell, New Mexico, the daughter of two people who enjoyed playing golf on weekends. Her parents began to take her along with them. By the time she was eight she was borrowing her mother's golf clubs,° following along behind her parents and trying to keep up with them. "The first lesson I ever had," Nancy has said, "was when my father

golf clubs

Nancy Lopez is one of the world's best golfers.

put the ball on the ground one day and told me to hit it into the hole way down there."°

way... far away

Nancy kept hitting and improving, and before long she could beat most of the women players in New Mexico. She kept on improving as she got older, and her parents realized what a great talent° she had. They decided to pay her expenses for practice and for travel to golf tournaments° all around the country.

special and unusual skill

games in which many players take part

A champion and wealthy by the time she was twenty-one, she is also very pretty and much more admired by sports fans° than most people in professional sports—male or female—ever are.

people interested in sports

Many people think that Nancy Lopez has an easy life. But she too has problems. "Probably the thing that I think about most is my personal life," she says. "It's very important for me to be with the people I want to be with." Now that she is married, Nancy knows that her family and home are more important to

Nancy's husband attends many of her tournaments.

in . . . over a long time

her than golf in the long run,° and she knows that being away at tournaments much of the time could hurt her family life. She has said that she would like to go on playing golf as long as she can do it well—perhaps another ten years—but she has also said that she may decide to retire in another few years in order to spend most of her time raising a family. It will surely be a difficult decision to make. But for now, Nancy Lopez will just keep on playing hard—and winning.

[467 words]

Adapted from *The Saturday Evening Post*

EXERCISES

Vocabulary **A** *Which of the following sentences is closest in meaning to the model?*

1. It is probably true that golf is popular because people like Nancy.
   a) It is probable that golf is popular because people like Nancy.
   b) It is true that golf is popular because people like Nancy.
   c) It is possible that golf is popular because people like Nancy.

2. In a few short years, Nancy Lopez has become a champion.
   a) After a few years, Nancy Lopez has become a champion again.
   b) Nancy Lopez became a champion in a few years.
   c) Shortly, Nancy Lopez will become a champion for a few years.

3. They are not sure about it.
   a) They know it isn't true.
   b) They think it may not be true.
   c) They are sure it isn't false.

4. What she thinks about most is her personal life.
   a) Mostly she thinks about her own life.
   b) She thinks about people in her life.
   c) She thinks about most people.

5. They began taking her along with them.
   a) They used to take her along with them.
   b) They took her along with them in the beginning.
   c) They started to take her along with them.

6. Nancy followed along behind her parents.
   a) Nancy walked a long time behind her parents.
   b) Her parents walked in front, and then came Nancy.
   c) Nancy walked along while her parents went behind her.
7. She was better than ever.
   a) She had never been better.
   b) She got better every time.
   c) She was always better.
8. Nancy planned to retire soon after she got married.
   a) Nancy's plans were to retire soon after she got married.
   b) Now that she has gotten married, Nancy may soon retire.
   c) Soon after she got married, Nancy planned to retire.

B *Complete the sentence with a word or expression from the article.*

1. A _____ person is one many people like.
2. Most people don't play golf on weekdays; they play on _____.
3. Nancy asked her mother if she could _____ one of her clubs.
4. We are not sure, but it is _____ true that Nancy Lopez will be playing again next year.
5. Nancy used to play golf only for fun, but now that she makes a living from the game she is considered a _____.
6. At first, her parents did not realize that Nancy had a great _____ for golf.
7. Golf and baseball are both popular _____ in America.
8. A golf ball is supposed to be hit into a _____.

C *Choose the most accurate of the three statements.*

1. To do something in the long run is
   a) to get there before anyone else does.
   b) to take a long time before doing something.
   c) to do it over a long period of time.
2. An athlete is
   a) a professional golfer.
   b) a person who plays a sport very often.
   c) a woman who is a champion.
3. A tournament is
   a) an important game.
   b) a weekend game.
   c) a woman's game.
4. Nancy's skill is
   a) her personality.
   b) her ability.
   c) her popularity.

5. To keep on improving is to
   a) look nicer and nicer.
   b) be happier and happier.
   c) get better and better.
6. To raise a family is to
   a) have children.
   b) be married.
   c) bring happiness.
7. Way down there is
   a) not far from here.
   b) not near there.
   c) not near here.
8. That she has made her decision means that
   a) she decided to make something.
   b) she will surely find it difficult.
   c) she now knows what she is going to do.

Structures

A She got married. She now makes another person happy. →
   Since getting married, she has made another person happy.

1. She had a lesson. She now plays better.
2. Her brother came to the golf course. Her brother now sees her play.
3. Nancy followed her parents. Nancy now begins to hit the ball well.
4. She traveled to golf tournaments. She now thinks of herself as a champion.
5. She became a champion. She now seems very popular.
6. He beat the champion. He now tries to be nice to people.
7. She borrowed her mother's club. She now never misses the ball.
8. He started to play. He now tires of the game.

B "I enjoy playing golf." → **She said she enjoyed playing golf.**

1. "I haven't always been happy."
2. "I used to walk behind my parents."
3. "My parents paid for me to go to tournaments."
4. "I don't really smile when I lose."
5. "I used to beat children my own age."
6. "My brothers and sisters watch me play."
7. "I started playing when I was seven."
8. "My father gave me my first lesson."

C She practices each day. → **She keeps on practicing each day.**

1. She smiles during the game.
2. She improves each year.

Nancy's father gave her the first golf lesson she ever had.

3. She plays in every tournament.
4. She follows her parents.
5. She wins all the games.
6. She talks to the children.
7. She hits the ball well.
8. She takes her sister with her.

Questions

1. In what year was Nancy Lopez born?
2. Where did Nancy first begin playing golf?
3. When did her parents play golf?
4. What is most important to Nancy Lopez in the long run?
5. How much longer is he likely to play very well?
6. In what way is Nancy different from many other champions?
7. Who gave Nancy her first golf lesson?
8. At what age did Nancy start playing golf?

Discussion

1. What are some good points and bad points about young children spending time playing sports?
2. Some sports professionals make more money than doctors, teachers, and even presidents. Do you think this is fair? Why or why not?

Cross-cultural Topic

In your country, do women have much chance to become famous in sports? Which sports do women play there? What do most people think of women athletes? Is there any woman as famous as Nancy Lopez? How would you compare her personality to Nancy's?

The Neighborhood Luncheonette

smaller

expression
in
French.

7

Marty's Luncheonette,° at 232 Sherman Avenue, near 207th Street in New York City, is long and narrow, with light brown walls and a white counter° with fourteen seats. Marty Rubin and his wife, Esther, have owned Marty's for more than twenty-five years. Most of the customers° live or work in the neighborhood and come to the restaurant because of Esther Rubin's good cooking.

Marty Rubin opens up the restaurant every morning at 7:30 A.M. He and Esther's sister, Gussie Markowitz, take care of the customers at breakfast. At 10:30 A.M., Marty leaves for his house in Yonkers to get Esther, who has spent the morning in her kitchen cooking the food.

small restaurant usually serving only breakfast and lunch

long bar at which people sit and eat

people who buy things

The counter has seats
for fourteen people.

At 11:40 A.M., one day not long ago, there were only four people at the counter. Five minutes later, all fourteen seats were filled. From 11:45 A.M. until 1:30 P.M., the counter was full and there were always two or three people standing and waiting for a seat to be empty.

During that hour and three-quarters, Marty, Esther, and Gussie didn't stop moving. Marty was at the cash register° and made cold drinks. Esther and Gussie served the food and the coffee and made sandwiches. The customers came in, ordered their food, waited quietly, ate quickly, paid, and left. The people were

cash . . . machine where
money is kept

neighborhood

friendly and most of them seemed to know each other. Many have come to Marty's every day for fifteen years.

Marty's

From about 1:45 P.M. until 5:30 P.M., when Marty's closes, there is not much business. Marty, Esther, and Gussie have their own lunches and prepare for the next day. One day a woman who formerly lived° in an apartment in the neighborhood before she moved to New Jersey came in for a cup of coffee at two o'clock. "I wish I could move back here," she said. "Where I live now, all the people are so busy with their own houses that they have no time to talk or be friendly. There's no place like Marty's. I miss it."°

formerly . . . had lived

I . . . I'm sorry I'm not here anymore

[323 words]

Adapted from *The New Yorker*

neighborhood

EXERCISES

A *Complete the sentence with a word or expression from the article.* **Vocabulary**

Neighborhood

1. People who live in the _____ come to the restaurant. → *narrow*
2. Marty's Luncheonette is long and NARROW *present. Time clause* *Povable Verbs.* *Time clause*
3. The customers **order** their food and then wait until it is served. — *order*
4. Esther has **spent** the morning in her kitchen. *Spent*
5. Marty's Luncheonette serves **breakfast** and lunch. — *breakfast*
6. Most of the customers **seem** to know each other. — *seem* *Filled Seem*
7. All the seats were **filled**. *Filled*
8. I **miss** Marty's place now that I live in New Jersey. — *miss* *Miss*

B *Which sentence best illustrates the use of the word or phrase in italics?*

1. The counter was *long* and narrow.
   a) It won't be long until Marty returns.
   b) How long is that street?
   c) He longs to return to the restaurant. *long* — *long* — *long to feel* *right morning* *long lose* *Dismissed* *Class*
2. Gussie *cares for* the customers at breakfast.
   a) She can't take care of the restaurant by herself.
   b) I don't care for this sandwich.
   c) He doesn't have a care in the world. *care for* *care for* *Grandmother* *Girlfriend*

Gussie and Marty run the luncheonette in the mornings.

3. Marty *leaves* for his house in Yonkers.
   a) She left the restaurant after lunch.
   b) The leaves fell off the tree.
   c) He turned left when he reached Yonkers.

4. I wish I could *move* back here.
   a) They didn't stop moving.
   b) She moved to New Jersey.
   c) Her movements were very quick.

5. Esther *served* the hot food.
   a) The drinks were served in the living room.
   b) There are three servants in the house.
   c) The luncheonette serves a need in the neighborhood.

6. Please *pass* the sugar.
   a) The days pass slowly.
   b) Can you pass that car?
   c) Will you pass me those things?

7. She *used to* live near Marty's.
   a) He can't get used to New Jersey.
   b) They used to have breakfast at 7:30.
   c) The cash register is no use to me.

8. He *made* the sandwiches.
   a) He made a quick movement.
   b) She made a lot of money.
   c) I made a small table.

A   Did they stop moving?   →
      STUDENT 1: **Yes, they stopped moving.**
      STUDENT 2: **No, they didn't stop moving.**

1.   Did he return to the restaurant early?   *Yes, he returned to the restaurant early*
                                               no, he didn't return to the restaurant early
2.   Did she have a cup of coffee?
3.   Did they prepare for the next day?   *yes, they prepared for the next day*
4.   Did the woman move to New Jersey?   *no they didn't prepare for the next day*
5.   Did she miss the neighborhood?
6.   Did they sit at the counter?
7.   Did the luncheonette look busy?
8.   Did Marty come late that day?

B   Marty's is the best luncheonette.   →
      There's no luncheonette like Marty's!

1.   Summer is the best season.   *There's no best season like summer.*
2.   Coffee is the best drink.   *There's no drink like coffee*
3.   Yonkers is the best place.   *There's no place like Yonkers*
4.   New York is the best city.   *There's no city like New York*

Marty pours the
breakfast coffee.

5. The lady from New Jersey is the best customer.
6. Gussie is the best sandwich maker.
7. Sherman Avenue is the best neighborhood.
8. Esther is the best cook.

C Formerly she lived in this neighborhood. →
She used to live in this neighborhood.

1. Formerly Marty's Luncheonette had ten seats.
2. Formerly people went there for breakfast.
3. Formerly the neighbors were friendly.
4. Formerly the walls were white.
5. Formerly Marty served the hot food.
6. Formerly they knew each other.
7. Formerly she lived in New York.
8. Formerly she had time to talk.

D It's a *luncheonette in the neighborhood.* →
It's a neighborhood luncheonette.

1. It's a *cup for coffee.*
2. Those are *people who are friendly.*
3. The *number of the street* is 207th.
4. Now it's *time for lunch.*
5. I don't like *drinks that are cold* in the winter.
6. She has *neighbors who are quiet.*
7. The *home of his family* is in Yonkers.
8. I want a *soda made with ice cream.*

True or False

Correct the sentence if it is false according to the article.

F 1. Gussie is Marty's sister. Gussie is Esther's sister.
F 2. The restaurant opens at 10:30 A.M. The restaurant opens at 7:30 a.m
T 3. Marty's Luncheonette is very busy at 12:30 P.M.
T 4. Esther Rubin is a good cook.
F 5. The woman from New Jersey came in while the restaurant was busy. The woman from New Jersey came in at 2:00 o'clock
F 6. Most of Marty's customers live in New Jersey. They live in New York
F 7. The customers do not talk to each other. - Customers seem to know each other
F 8. The people in New Jersey have time to talk and be friendly. They are so busy they don't have time to talk.

Questions

1. During what hours is Marty's Luncheonette open? 7:30 – 5:30 p.m.
2. Where do Marty and Esther live? Yonkers

3. How many people can eat at Marty's at the same time? *14 people*
4. Why wasn't Esther in the restaurant at breakfast? *She was in her kitchen cooking food*
5. Who makes the sandwiches at lunch time? *Esther and Gussie.*
6. Where do most customers who go to Marty's come from? *They work or live there.*
7. Why does the woman from New Jersey like Marty's? *because people are friendly.*
8. How does the woman feel about Marty's place? *She misses it*

Discussion

1. Is the real life of a big city found in its large business buildings and in its crowded streets, or in its small stores and neighborhoods?
2. Why would people who have their own houses spend less time talking with their neighbors than people who live in apartment houses?

Imagination

Three students play the roles of customers who all go to eat at Marty's luncheonette at the same time. Another student plays the role of Marty or Gussie and takes their orders. They discuss such things as the weather and the quality of the food. The customers should not forget to pay.

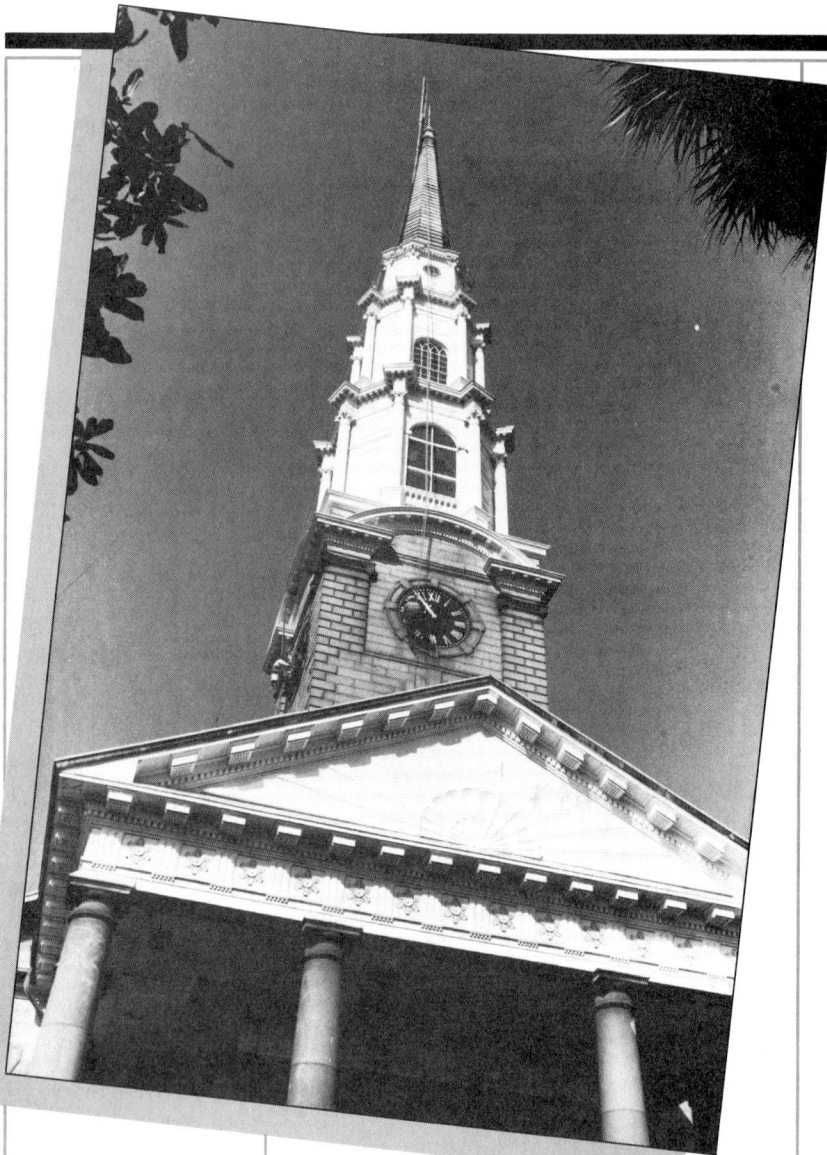

8

A Family
of Steeplejacks

Are you afraid of heights?° Do you feel dizzy° when you look down at the ground from a high place? If you do, you have nothing to be ashamed of.° Most people have some fear of being far up above the earth. Most people—but not the O'Neil family. Jerry O'Neil and his wife Beverly, their sons Darrell and Tim, and the sons' wives, Judy and Linda, all work as steeplejacks—people who paint and fix church roofs and clocks and steeples, the highest parts of tall church buildings.

As time goes by, many old church buildings become damaged by wind, rain, and snow. The roofs begin to leak,° the paint peels, and the decorations—many of them beautifully made many years ago—begin to wear out.° The church members then decide to hire° someone to make the repairs. Because the stee-

places high above the
ground / not steady

ashamed . . . feeling that
you have done something
wrong

dizzy

let water come through

wear . . . become less
usable because of age
employ

Beverly O'Neil puts new gold leaf on the numbers from the old church clock.

ples are so tall, repairing them from the ground can be very expensive. It is cheaper to work from the top of the steeple down than from the ground up! And that is exactly what the O'Neil family does.

To do their work, the O'Neils have to sit on seats that hang down from ropes attached to the very tops of the church steeples. If you watch them at work, you can see them swinging gently in midair while they repair a roof or replace the old numbers on a church clock with newly painted ones.

have . . . not be afraid

Would you have the nerve° to do that kind of work? Probably not—most people wouldn't. That's why there aren't very many

Seated high above the ground, Darrell O'Neil goes about his unusual work.

steeplejacks. That is also why the O'Neil family seems to be busy all year long and why they are called to work in many parts of the country.

The O'Neils not only enjoy working together; they like the freedom of traveling around the country and finding jobs as they go. The group drives in three trailers, three trucks, and a car. Jerry and Beverly O'Neil have just bought a new 40-foot trailer. "I live in a house I pull behind me," Beverly said.

Although she does not yet work with them, six-year-old Rachel, Darrell and Judy's daughter, goes everywhere with the family. She even gets her education on the road, taking a cor-respondence course° instead of attending regular school. The whole family has adapted to° the traveling life. In fact, they enjoy it so much that they invite their friends and relatives to share it by celebrating Christmas with them in the trailers.

The O'Neils like heights so much that Tim took Linda up into a church steeple to propose.° But even though they make climbing steeples look easy, the O'Neils know that it is danger-ous, and they are very careful. "Accidents don't happen by them-selves," says Tim. "Someone causes them. We all know that, and that is why we are always watching and helping each other. But so far," he added, "the only things we've broken are a few of our fingernails."°

correspondence . . .
school lessons through
the mail

adapted . . . gotten used to

ask her to marry him

fingernails

[498 words]

Adapted from *The New York Times*

EXERCISES

(A) *Complete the sentence with a word or expression from the article.*   **Vocabulary**

1. Places far above the ground are called ___heights___   *vergustado*
2. Many of us are ___ashamed___ to let people know that we are afraid of something.   *Sabe*
3. I wouldn't have ___the nerve___ to do that kind of work.

4. It costs less to do the work from the top of the steeple. It is _cheaper_ to do it that way.
5. Their work does not seem to be difficult. They make it _looks easy_.
6. They travel almost all the time. They are _on_ the _road_ all year.
7. She cannot go to a _regular_ school, the kind other children go to.
8. He is sitting in _midair_, between the top of the building and the ground.

B *In your own words, what is*

1. a trailer?
2. a fear?
3. a steeple?
4. a steeplejack?
5. a relative?
6. a dangerous job?
7. an accident?
8. a repair?

C *Fill the blank in each of the following sentences with a noun suggested by the verb in parentheses.*

1. The _painter_ was working near the top of the church. (paint)
2. Most of the _decorators_ were beginning to wear out. (decorate)
3. All those _workers_ are in the same family. (work)
4. We have the _freedom_ to find our own jobs. (free)
5. His _propose_ as made in an unusual place. (propose)
6. They think their _traveling_ makes their lives more interesting. (travel)
7. The _repairs_ to the steeples are usually expensive. (repair)
8. Lots of _damage_ is caused by wind, rain, and snow. (damage)

Questions

1. Why don't Darrell and Judy send their daughter to a regular school?
2. How can the church members save money when their church building needs repair?
3. Why is a steeplejack's job dangerous?
4. Why is it less expensive to repair steeples from the top than from the ground?
5. Why aren't there many steeplejacks?
6. What do the O'Neils do to prevent accidents?
7. What does "Accidents don't happen by themselves" mean?
8. In what ways is the O'Neil family different from most other families? Name at least four ways.

Structures

A I don't have much money. I have a job. →
I don't have much money but I do have a job.

1. He doesn't have a car. He has a truck.
2. Rachel doesn't go to a regular school. She takes a correspondence course.
3. Most people don't do that kind of work. They like to watch it.
4. The O'Neils don't stay in one place. They have a Christmas party.
5. Linda doesn't like heights. She wants to work with her husband.
6. I don't work near the ground. I climb down from the top of the buildings.
7. We don't want other people to know about it. We are afraid of heights.
8. The buildings don't look very old. They need many repairs.

B   How do you paint a steeple? Just call a steeplejack.   →
    To paint a steeple, all you have to do is call a steeplejack.

1. How do you take a correspondence course? Just send for the lessons.
2. How do you hang in midair? Just attach the ropes from the roof.
3. How do you travel so much? Just buy a trailer.
4. How do you find a job? Just look for a church that needs painting.
5. How do you stop accidents? Just watch and help each other.
6. How do you propose to a steeplejack? Just take her up into the steeple.
7. How do you make the work cheaper? Just do it from the top down.
8. How do you make climbing steeples look easy? Just close your eyes.

C   Should we paint it or fix it?   →
    We want either to paint or to fix it.

1. Should we repair it or replace it?
2. Should the O'Neils rent a trailer or buy a truck?
3. Should Rachel go to a regular school or take a correspondence course?
4. Should they stay on the road or stop and have a party?
5. Should we watch the steeplejacks or go inside the church?
6. Should Darrell fix the clock or climb up to the roof?
7. Should he do that work or find an easier job?
8. Should the man look down at the ground or stop the seat from swinging?

Points of View

1. Would you rather have a job that is very safe, or one that is a little dangerous? Why?
2. How do you think children feel if their families have to move frequently? Why? What are some advantages and disadvantages for children of moving frequently?

Cross-cultural Topics

1. If a family drove into a city in your country in three trailers, three trucks, and a car, what would most people think about them? Would they be able to find work? Would it make any difference if there weren't any small children in the family? Why or why not?
2. Suppose you were a member of such a family. How would you explain your life to the people of that city?

Dear Abby

9

Sometimes, when people have problems they cannot solve by themselves, they write to a newspaper columnist° like Abigail Van Buren, who calls herself Abby. She prints some of the letters in her column and adds her own advice or comments.

someone who always writes about the same general subject

a group of persons who decide what is true in a law trial

DEAR ABBY: I was called to serve on a jury° and was really looking forward to serving, but when I told my husband, he said: "You *have* to get out of it!" I asked him why, and he couldn't give me a good reason; he just demanded that I try to get out of it.

Abby, I think it would be a good experience for me. Furthermore, I consider it my duty. My children are in school, and it wouldn't be difficult for me to find the time.

I know you are in favor of keeping peace in the family, but I honestly think my husband is wrong to demand that I get out of serving on a jury. So how do I defend my point of view?

CITIZEN°

member of a country by birth or law

judged

Declaration ... formal announcement of the United States' freedom from England (July 4th, 1776)

DEAR CITIZEN: You're right when you say it is your duty. I hope your husband never gets in trouble with the law, but ask him how he'd feel if he were tried° by a judge alone because all his neighbors and fellow citizens refused to serve on a jury.

Then tell him to reread the Declaration of Independence,° and to remember that one of the complaints of the first Americans against King George of England was that they were not permitted to have jury trials. If your husband continues to refuse you the right to serve on a jury, declare your independence on this point. It is one of the only two public services a citizen is asked to perform; the other is voting.

DEAR ABBY: I will never again say that a letter I read in your column is too unbelievable to be real. Listen to this:

My husband and I recently attended the twenty-fifth anniversary party° of a married couple we had known for years. It was a beautiful dinner party, held at a fancy restaurant, with about one hundred guests attending.

twenty-fifth ... celebration of twenty-five years of marriage

Around midnight, the husband said that he and his wife had an announcement to make. They stood together, and he said: "We've had twenty-five years of marriage. Our children are married now, and there is no longer any reason to go on pretending our marriage is a success. It has been a failure for many years, so we've decided that while we are both young enough to enjoy life, we're getting divorced.° It's nobody's fault. It's friendly and mutual° and we hope you will continue to be our friends."

getting ... separating, ending the marriage
agreed upon by both persons

They kissed each other and danced together as the band played "Good Night, Sweetheart."

At first we all thought it was a joke.° It wasn't! They asked those who had brought gifts to please keep them, saying they had decided only yesterday to announce their divorce at their anniversary party since all their friends would be there.

something to make people laugh

Has anyone ever heard anything stranger than this?

WAS THERE

DEAR WAS: I hope not.

[515 words]

Adapted from *Dear Abby*

EXERCISES

Word Families

STUDENT 1: What does that woman do all day? →
STUDENT 2: **She works. She's a worker.**
STUDENT 1: What is she doing right now? →
STUDENT 2: **She's working.**

Repeat for: **teach, dance, write, paint, read, worry, advise, judge.**

Vocabulary

A *Choose the most accurate of the three statements.*

1. If you cannot do something by yourself,
   a) you need help.
   b) you cannot get help.
   c) you cannot get help yourself.
2. If you serve on a jury,
   a) you work for the jury.
   b) you speak to the jury.
   c) you are part of the jury.
3. If you are looking forward to something,
   a) you can see it happening.
   b) you are waiting for it to happen.
   c) it is happening in front of you.
4. If a man keeps peace, he is
   a) demanding less action.
   b) serving both sides.
   c) preventing a fight.
5. Your fellow citizens are
   a) other citizens of your country.
   b) other fellows from your country.
   c) other people you knew in your country.
6. If two people stand together, they are
   a) working together.
   b) married.
   c) keeping the peace.
7. If it's nobody's fault, it's
   a) not his fault.
   b) his fault but not their fault.
   c) not his fault, but it could be their fault.
8. If you've never heard anything stranger,
   a) you've heard nothing.
   b) you've heard nothing stranger.
   c) you've heard something even stranger.

Failure.

B *Complete the sentence with a word or expression from the article.*

1. He explained it very well. He gave very good reason for it.
2. I believed I had to do it. I consider it my duty.
3. He tried to resolve the problem, but couldn't find an answer.
4. Voting and serving on a jury are two public services.
5. The marriage had been a failure for years, but no one had expected them to get a divorce.
6. They were serious about it. It was not a joke.
7. We have been friends for years and we will continue to be friends.
8. The Americans didn't like King George. They had many complaints against him.

A He says serving on a jury will waste her time. →
He said serving on a jury would waste her time.

Structures

1. He says getting excused will be better.
2. He asks if she will give it up.
3. She knows it will be a good experience.
4. She thinks he will change his mind.
5. We pretend the marriage will work.
6. They ask if we will take the gifts home.
7. I want to see if they will dance together.
8. She announces what they will do.

B I want to defend my point of view. →
She can't defend her point of view, so how can I?

1. I want to keep peace with my husband.
2. I want to serve on the jury.
3. I want to attend the party.
4. I want to take the gifts home.
5. I want to write a letter to Abby.
6. I want to declare my independence.
7. I want to give him a good reason.
8. I want to continue to be his friend.

Retell the following passage as if it happened long ago. Begin: "Years ago, I was the husband . . ."

Time Change

I am the husband of the woman who calls herself "Citizen," and I insist that it is not right for her to be away from home when the children and I need her. Each day, we all wake up together, eat breakfast together, and talk for a while before going to school or to the office. I am afraid she will have to leave the house very early to serve on the jury. I think I am right to ask her to get out of it. She disagrees with me very strongly.

Questions

1. Why does "Citizen" want to serve on a jury?
2. What does her husband want her to do?
3. Will her children need her at home?
4. Which two duties does every American citizen have?
5. How many guests attended the anniversary party?
6. How did the guests feel when they heard the announcement?
7. Why was the divorce announced at the anniversary party?
8. Whose fault was it that the couple was getting divorced?

Write a Letter

Pretend that you are Abby. You receive a letter from a husband and wife who say that they are not happy together and are only continuing their marriage because of their small children. Answer the letter, giving your advice.

Personal Opinion

What do you think of newspaper columns like Dear Abby? Do they serve a useful purpose? Should people like Abby who give advice have special training? Should they have to take a test?

Cross-cultural Topic

Think about the couple who announced their divorce on their twenty-fifth anniversary. Could such a thing happen in your country? If not, why not?

Farm-rest.

10
Aquaculture: New Hope for Food

Oysters are grown on nylon strings that hang from metal racks.

oyster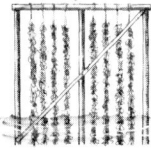

gathered, collected

good tasting

age group

rack

change, turn around / methods, ways

Aquaculture—or sea farming, as it is sometimes called—is one of the brightest hopes for finding an answer to the problem of a world food shortage. Although it may be years before aquaculture yields really large quantities of food, it is already partially successful. One of its successes is the growing of oysters.°

Oyster farming is a big new business on Cape Cod, where large crops of oysters have been harvested.° The waters there were famous for delicious° oysters until the supply gave out about fifteen years ago. "There's a whole generation° of people who have never eaten oysters," says Karl Touraine, marketing director of Aqua Dynamics Corporation, a company that grows oysters on strings hanging from metal racks.° "For about twenty years the oyster has been in short supply, and our aim is to reverse° this by using new, modern growing techniques,"° he explains.

"Wareham, on Cape Cod, is the first place in the United States where oysters are being grown on racks just off the bottom of the sea," says Hank McAvoy of the National Marine Fisheries Service in Gloucester. "But there's nothing new about off-bottom raising," Mr. McAvoy adds. "It's been done successfully in Norway and Australia and, in the last few years, in Spain. The Japanese have used this form of aquaculture for years, and they're the most successful, with a yearly crop of more than forty-six thousand pounds of shelled oysters to the acre."°

land measure: 43,560 square feet

The Aqua Dynamics group grows oysters on strings, away from the bottom so that the oysters' natural enemies cannot reach them. "When an oyster can avoid° enemies and live in unpolluted° water with plenty to eat, he'll grow fat in four years," Karl Touraine explains. "Oysters will attach themselves to almost anything they can," he continues. "At Wareham, we use shells, which we tie with nylon strings hanging from metal racks. We lower the strings into the water, leaving at least a foot of water between the lowest shell and the bottom."

keep away from

pure, clean

"So far the growth has been excellent and the taste just delightful," Mr. Touraine notes happily.

[347 words]

Adapted from *The Christian Science Monitor*

EXERCISES

Vocabulary

A Complete the sentence with a word or expression from the article.

1. The shortage of oysters has been turned around; it has been _____
2. If something has been done before, there's _____ new about it.
3. The supply ended; it _____ _____.
4. Oysters grow well in clean, or _____ waters.
5. There has been excellent growth until now; that is, the growth has been excellent _____ _____.
6. The taste is very good; it's _____.
7. There is not enough food for everyone; there is a food _____.
8. The method has worked well in Norway and Australia; they have been _____ with it.

Aquaculture produces millions of pounds of food each year.

B *Choose the most accurate of the three statements.*

1. A crop of oysters is
   a) a kind of successful aquaculture.
   b) what was harvested.
   c) one of the metal racks used on Cape Cod.

2. Sea farming is a bright hope to end the food shortage.
   a) It is used all over the world.
   b) It is an old method.
   c) It is likely to help to solve the problem.

3. Unpolluted water
   a) does not help the oysters.
   b) does not help the oyster growers.
   c) helps the oysters grow fat.

4. A delicious oyster is
   a) good to eat.
   b) lower on the string.
   c) four years old.

5. It yielded many oysters.
   a) It stopped them.
   b) It produced them.
   c) It lost them.

6. The oyster's natural enemies are found
   a) in the supply.
   b) in the market.
   c) in the sea.
7. A shelled oyster
   a) fastens itself to the string.
   b) does not have a shell.
   c) is lowered into the water.
8. The quantity of oysters is
   a) the length of them. *tvduno - lovyo - Extension*
   b) the size of them.
   c) the number of them.

Antonyms

Write the antonyms (opposites) for the following words, using **im-** or **un-**. *Example = possible — impossible (one word)*

1. polluted – *Unpolluted*   5. do *Undo*   *look in the*
2. perfect – *imperfect*   6. pure *impure*   *Dictionary*
3. successful *unsuccessful*   7. yielding *unyielding*
4. fasten *Unfasten*   8. partial *impartial*

Structures

A When will the new method be tried? →
   It has already been tried.

1. When will the people be fed?
2. When will the problems be solved?
3. When will the first crop be harvested?
4. When will the curve be reversed?
5. When will the method be found?
6. When will the oysters be shelled?
7. When will the racks be lowered?
8. When will the strings be tied?

B Oysters are usually grown on Cape Cod. →
   However, they have not been grown on Cape Cod this year.

1. Oysters are usually hung from metal racks.
2. Oysters are usually sold cheaply.
3. The water is usually polluted.
4. The farmers are usually successful.
5. The oysters are usually large and delicious.
6. Shells are usually tied far apart.
7. The strings are usually covered with shells.
8. The oysters' enemies are usually able to reach them.

C   Aquaculture is a bright hope for food. →
Aquaculture is one of the brightest hopes for food.

1. Using metal racks is a new method of growing oysters.
2. Oyster farming is a big business on Cape Cod.
3. Aqua Dynamics is a large sea-farming company.
4. This shell is a hard thing to break.
5. Wareham is a small town on Cape Cod.
6. The off-bottom method is an old form of aquaculture.
7. Sea farming is an easy way to raise food.
8. An oyster is a good food to eat.

D   The oyster couldn't avoid its enemies. →
The oyster couldn't have avoided its enemies before, but it is avoiding them now.

1. The Japanese couldn't grow many oysters.
2. He couldn't tie the shells.
3. The sea farmer couldn't use the off-bottom method.
4. The oysters couldn't attach themselves to strings.
5. Aquaculture couldn't be done successfully in Norway.
6. A whole generation couldn't eat oysters.
7. Hank couldn't lower the string into the water.
8. The supply couldn't give out.

Oyster shells hang on the side of a building in Cape Cod.

Follow this example: bright → **brighter** → **brightest**   **Comparisons**

1. large
2. new
3. short
4. few
5. nice
6. fat
7. low
8. tasty

Correct the sentence if it is false according to the article.   **True or False**

1. The oysters hang on strings.
2. Mr. Touraine works in Japan.
3. Many people have never eaten oysters.
4. The off-bottom method was used in Wareham fifteen years ago.
5. The Aqua Dynamics Corporation sells metal racks.
6. Aquaculture has not yet solved the food problem.
7. The cleaner the water, the better the oyster.
8. The lower the string, the better the oyster.

Questions

1. Where do the oysters' enemies live?
2. How long does it take before an oyster is harvested?
3. In what countries had the off-bottom method been used?
4. For how long had Wareham been without oysters?
5. In what order are the following attached to each other: nylon strings, shells, metal racks, oysters?
6. Why have some people on Cape Cod never eaten oysters?
7. How far above the bottom must the oysters be?
8. What is Mr. Touraine's job?

Discussion

1. How can aquaculture help solve the world's food problems? What other crops can be grown underwater?
2. What other kinds of answers can we find to solve the world food problems? What can be done by farmers? By people who live in cities?

Personal Opinion

What kinds of food do you like best? Is there any kind of food you don't like? Why?

A Different Way to Get to Work

11

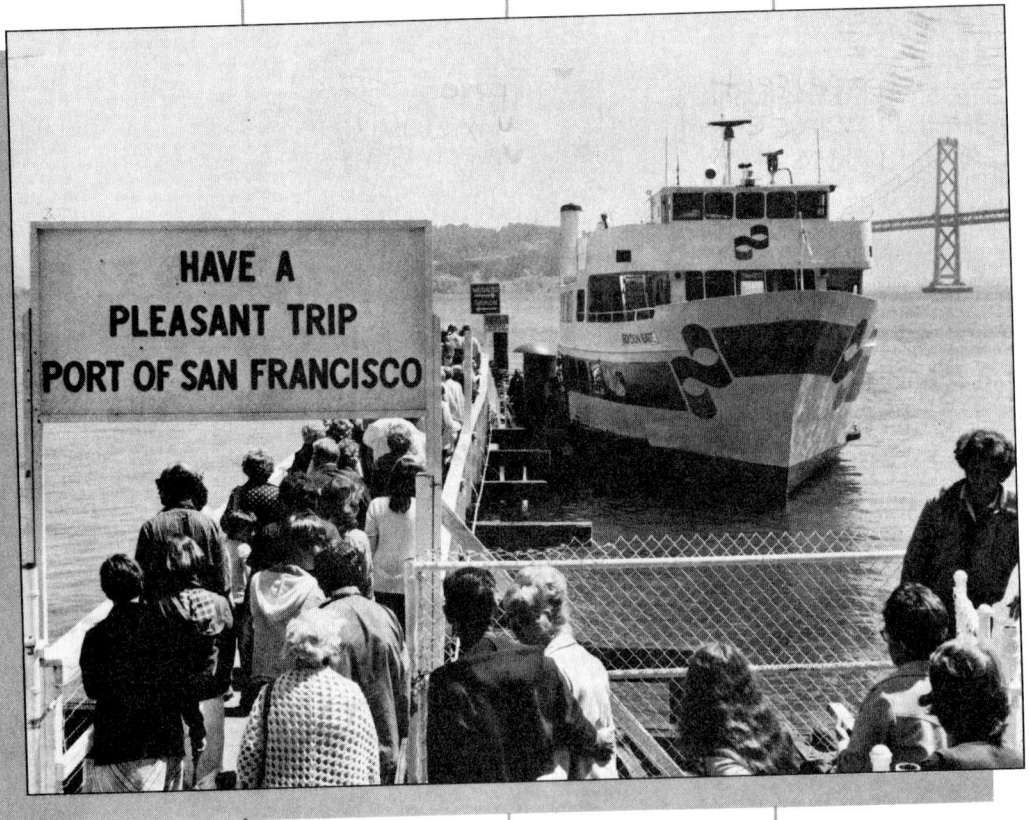

HAVE A
PLEASANT TRIP
PORT OF SAN FRANCISCO

The Golden Gate Bridge joins the beautiful city of San Francisco with the suburbs° to the north. Each day, about one hundred thousand automobiles cross the bridge, taking people to and from the city. More than half of them cross the bridge during the morning and evening rush hours;° with traffic so heavy, the trip is not pleasant.

Now, however, there is at least one group of happy commuters.° These are the people who travel under the bridge instead of on it. They go to work by boat and enjoy it so much that most of them say they will never go by car again.

The ferry° they take is the roomy, quiet, comfortable "Golden Gate." Commuters can enjoy the sun on deck.° In the morning they can have breakfast in the coffee shop, and in the

living areas near a city

rush . . . times when most people are going to and from work

people who travel back and forth regularly

boat that goes back and forth between two places
floor of a boat

Boats take commuters from the suburbs to the city.

evening they can order a drink in the bar while looking at San Francisco's famous skyline° and the nearby hills.

view of the city

The trip takes only thirty minutes and is not very costly. But best of all, being on a boat seems to make people feel more friendly toward each other. There has already been a marriage of two commuters who met on the "Golden Gate."

Because the ferry has been so successful, there are plans to use other, still larger boats. There is also a proposal° for a high-speed boat that will make the trip in only fifteen minutes.

plan

Not everyone is happy about that. "A lot of people don't want to get back and forth faster," said one commuter. "They feel that half an hour is just enough time to relax."

[267 words]

Based on a story from TIME, The Weekly Newsmagazine; Copyright Time Inc.

EXERCISES

Vocabulary

A *Choose the most accurate of the three statements.*

1. A hill is a
   a) small city.
   b) small mountain.
   c) small boat.
2. To take a trip is to travel
   a) from one place to another.
   b) during the morning and evening rush hours.
   c) for half an hour or more.
3. If more than half the people cross the bridge,
   a) more than half work in San Francisco.
   b) less than half go by car.
   c) less than half use the ferry.
4. A high-speed boat is
   a) faster than most cars.
   b) faster than most boats.
   c) faster than most traffic.
5. If not everyone is happy,
   a) not everyone is unhappy.
   b) more than half are unhappy.
   c) everyone is unhappy.

A hundred thousand automobiles cross the Golden Gate Bridge each day.

6. If half an hour is just enough time to relax, then
   a) fifteen minutes is time enough to relax.
   b) fifteen minutes is enough time to just relax.
   c) fifteen minutes is not enough time to relax.

7. If you do something while looking at something else,
   a) you are doing two things at once.
   b) you are doing something alone.
   c) you are doing it with your eyes closed.

8. If something is not very costly,
   a) it does not cost very much more than it used to.
   b) it does not cost very much less than it used to.
   c) it does not cost very much.

[handwritten in margin: Present / Commmuters]

[handwritten in margin: Friendly]

B   *Complete the sentence with a word or expression from the article.*

1. They enjoyed the trip very much. It was a *pleasure* to go to work.
2. One idea that has been suggested is to use larger boats. Another *proposal* is to use faster ones.
3. The *commuters* travel to work every morning and go back home every evening.
4. The bridge goes from San Francisco to the suburbs. It *joins* the two areas.
5. To go from one end of a bridge to the other is to *cross* the bridge.
6. The bridge isn't very far away. It is *near*
7. You feel rested and *friendly* after a trip on the ferry.
8. That's an unusual way to get to work. It certainly is a *different* way. *unusual*

Structures   **A**   People used to be more friendly. →
People used to be friendlier.

1. The trip will soon be more costly. *The trip will soon be costly*
2. The old ferry was more roomy. *The old ferry was roomier*
3. The new boat will be more speedy. *The new boat will be speedier*
4. But the people on it won't be ~~more~~ happy. *happier*
5. The traffic probably will be even ~~more~~ heavy. *heavier*
6. The deck is always ~~more sunny~~ *sunnier* than the inside rooms.
7. Traveling by boat is ~~more~~ pleasant than going by car.
8. The bar was ~~more~~ smoky than the coffee shop. *smokier*

B   You can drink coffee and also travel to work. →
You can drink coffee while traveling to work.

[handwritten in margin: while commuting]

1. A person can work in the city ~~and also live~~ in the country. *while living*
2. You can meet new people ~~and also~~ sit on deck. *while sitting*
3. Many people like to look at the skyline ~~and also have~~ a drink at the bar. *while having*
4. That couple got to know each other ~~and also commuted~~ to work.
5. It is difficult to enjoy the view ~~and also drive~~ a car. *while driving*
6. I can talk with friendly people ~~and also ride~~ to work. *while riding*
7. They love to see the city lights ~~and also~~ cross over to the suburbs at night. *while crossing*
8. Some commuters read newspapers ~~and also enjoy~~ the sun on deck. *while enjoying*

C   The traffic is heavy. The trip is no pleasure. →
With the traffic so heavy, the trip is no pleasure.

1. Commuting time is short. The ferry must move quickly.
2. The wind is strong. Newspapers are hard to hold.

Commuters like the boat because it gives them time to relax.

3. Everyone on the ferry is happy. Nobody thinks about work.
4. San Francisco's skyline is near. Hardly anyone looks toward the suburbs.
5. The Golden Gate Bridge is filled with cars. Lots of people think of commuting by boat.
6. The coffee shop is empty. More people are crowded on deck.
7. The new ferry is fast. The trip would be shorter.
8. The boat is full. The commuters are not happy.

Questions

1. Why were some people unhappy about commuting to work by car?
2. Which people are happy now?
3. What are the ferry's advantages?
4. Is the trip long and expensive?
5. In what ways do people act differently when they are on a boat?
6. What plans are being made for the future of the ferry?
7. Where can the commuters eat breakfast?
8. If a new bridge were built, would people still commute by boat?

Imagination

(for two students at a time)
Pretend that you live in the suburbs and are taking the ferry to work. You are sitting next to another commuter and want to talk to him or her. Hold a conversation for at least three minutes. You can talk about work, family, the view, the weather, the latest news, and so on.

Wondsday

12

The Real Jazz

At the beginning of this century,° a new music called jazz was
born in New Orleans. It was a "good time" music intended to
make people happy, but it was not so much a kind of music as a
style of playing. The New Orleans musicians learned to work
together to produce a loose, relaxed beat that is so powerful that
listeners cannot help but dance, or at least move their feet along
with it. The melody° is always clearly heard, sung by the different instruments° with a beautiful voicelike warmth. As one
player put it, the idea is to "play pretty for all the people."

instruments

A different band plays the old music each night in the run-down building.

At . . . around 1900

tune

in poor condition

The best—almost the only—place to hear the original New Orleans jazz is in Preservation Hall, a run-down° little building in the center of one of the city's most historic neighborhoods, the French Quarter. There seven different bands, made up mostly of very old men, play the old music for four and a half hours each evening. Some of the people in the audience are tourists, but most are serious music lovers who are willing to spend time sitting on plain wooden chairs and benches, and even on the floor. The musicians play the music they want to play, but people in the audience can make special requests° if they are willing to pay for them. Traditional songs cost one dollar and all others cost two—except the most traditional song of all, "The Saints." The musicians are so tired of playing it that it costs five dollars.

make . . . ask for a particular song

Old-style New Orleans jazz is in danger of disappearing because the men and women who can still play it are getting very old. Many of the players at Preservation Hall are well over seventy years old. The music did disappear once before, when

Jazz was born in New Orleans and born again in Preservation Hall.

Madera

Music lovers stand or sit on wooden benches to hear the old jazz.

people lost interest in it and the musicians had to make their
livings doing other things. But the current jazz revival° began in
1938, when music historian William Russell found the legend-
ary° trumpet player Bunk Johnson working in the fields and
brought him back to New Orleans to play. When Preservation
Hall opened in 1961, the old music finally had a place to live
again, and its popularity has grown ever since. Now groups from
the Hall travel all around the country, giving people their last
chance to hear music that will not exist for much longer, played
by the musicians who actually invented° it.

renewed interest

very famous in the past

made for the first time

[374 words]

Adapted from material supplied by Preservation Hall

EXERCISES

Vocabulary **A** *Choose the most accurate of the three statements.*

1. To move along with something is to
   a) walk toward it.
   b) keep in time with it.
   c) hear its melody.
2. A historic neighborhood is one in which
   a) history was made.
   b) history is being made.
   c) history will be made.
3. A person who is willing to do something
   a) is trying to do it.
   b) refuses to do it.
   c) agrees to do it.
4. If something is in danger of disappearing, it
   a) probably will disappear.
   b) cannot be seen anymore.
   c) is frightened of what it sees.
5. If someone makes a living, he or she
   a) is very old.
   b) is working.
   c) grows up.
6. If something has happened ever since 1961, it happened
   a) in 1964 and 1965, but not in 1962.
   b) in 1960 and 1961, but not in 1958.
   c) in 1963 and 1964, but not in 1957.
7. If you clearly hear somebody,
   a) you can also see him.
   b) you cannot also see him.
   c) you may or may not also see him.
8. If a man is well over 70 years old, he is most probably
   a) 79.
   b) 71.
   c) 70.

B *Complete the sentence with a word from the article.*

1. The tourists come from all over; they are _____ music lovers.
2. Preservation Hall is an old, _____ building.
3. They do not sit on metal chairs, but on _____ ones.
4. Preservation Hall is not a fancy place, so the people sit on _____ benches.
5. It started back in the early 1900s, at the beginning of the _____.

6. People had lost *interest* in the early jazz style. *Peoplidos*
7. Some people pay extra to hear *special* requests, in addition to those the musicians were going to play.
8. The shows *travel* around the country, taking jazz to the people.

travol

A STUDENT 1: Did they lose the music? →
   STUDENT 2: **Yes, the music was soon lost.**

1. Did they understand the style?
2. Did they forget the song?
3. Did they remember the trumpet player?
4. Did they bring back the old jazz?
5. Did they put back together the old groups?
6. Did they request the traditional songs?
7. Did they fill the hall?
8. Did they awaken our interest?

B STUDENT 1: Do they play this kind of music anywhere else? →
   STUDENT 2: **No, this is a kind of music played nowhere else.**

1. Do they do this kind of dance anywhere else?
2. Can one see this kind of show anywhere else?
3. Do they sing this kind of song anywhere else?
4. Do they use this kind of bench anywhere else?
5. Can one hear this kind of music anywhere else?
6. Can tourists enjoy this kind of place anywhere else?
7. Do old people make this kind of history anywhere else?
8. Can Russell find this kind of musician anywhere else?

C The tourists are music lovers. They go there from all over the world. →
   The tourists, many of them music lovers, go there from all over the world.

1. The songs are rarely heard. They are played only in New Orleans.
2. The musicians are very old. They earn more money than they used to.
3. The trumpets are quite new. They give out the old sounds.
4. The people are sitting on the floor. They love to hear the old jazz.
5. The shows are very popular. They travel all over the country.
6. The songs are of different kinds. They all sound the same.
7. The players are from New Orleans. They are about the same age.
8. The styles are no longer popular. They keep William Russell happy.

Serious
Plain
Wooden
Run-down
century
interest
Special
travel

1. In what part of New Orleans is Preservation Hall?
2. How old are the musicians?
3. Where was Bunk Johnson found?
4. How much does it cost to request a song at Preservation Hall?
5. Why will the old-style jazz be gone before long?
6. Where can you hear old-style jazz if you don't go to New Orleans?
7. Why do the musicians like to work in Preservation Hall?
8. Why do you think the old-style jazz had been forgotten?

Discussion

What differences are there between those people who like classical music and those who like the music played at Preservation Hall? Could the same people like both kinds of music?

Cross-cultural topics

1. Are there different styles of music in your country? What are the differences between them? What kinds of people like each style?
2. Jazz is called America's own music because it began here and spread throughout the world. Is jazz heard in your country? Is any other kind of American music heard there? What effect has American music had on the music in your country?

Marriage: American Style

13

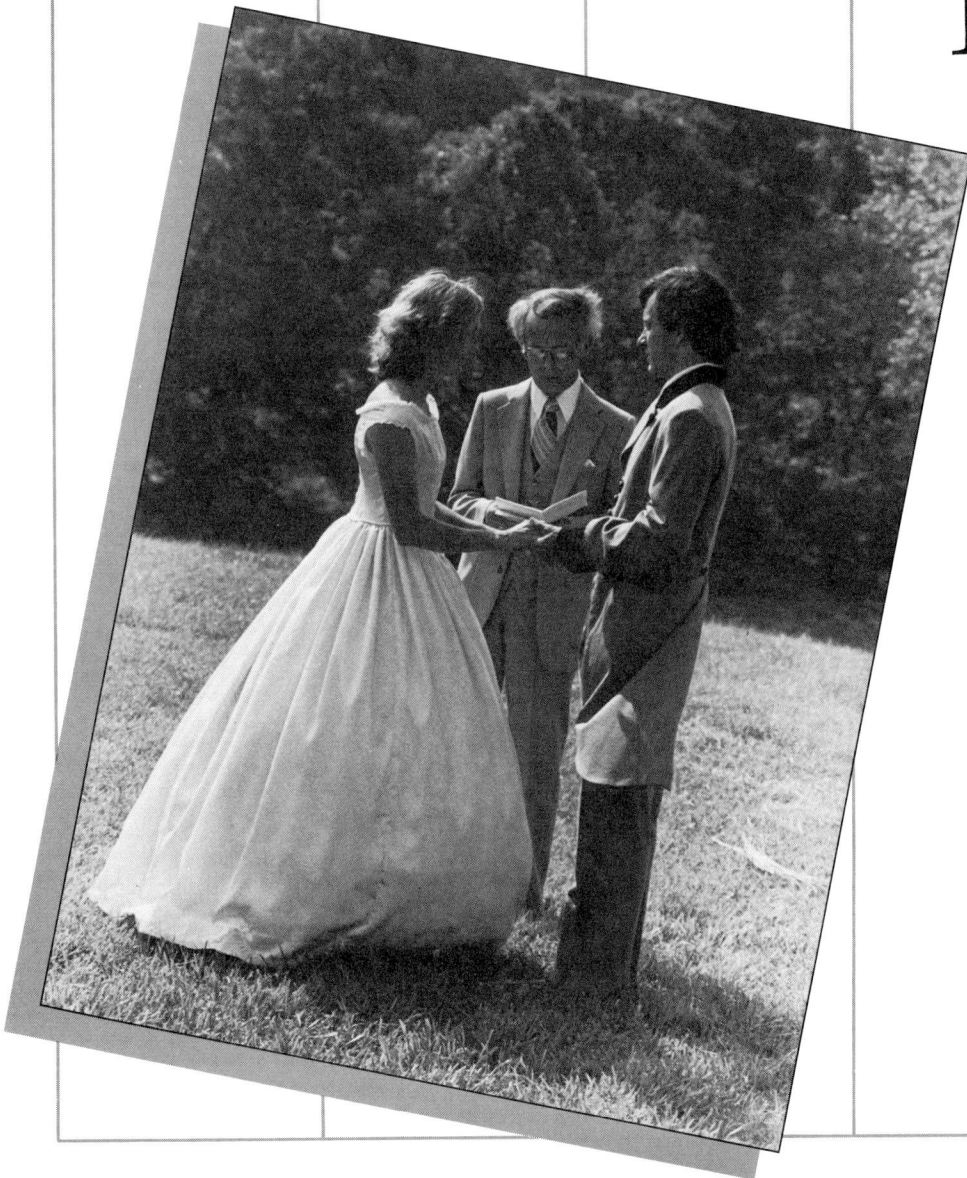

Eugene Epstein first went to the Griffith Park Planetarium° in Los Angeles when he was five years old; his visit interested him so much that he later became an astronomer.° The first time he met Carol Schiller he invited her to the planetarium and together they looked through a telescope° at the stars and planets. When

roller coaster

planetarium

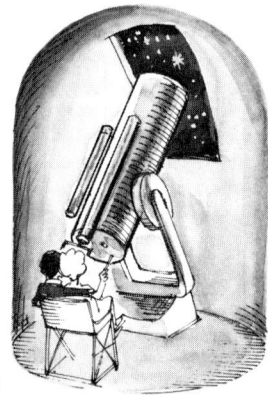

telescope

Carol and Eugene recently decided to get married, it did not seem unusual to them to have the wedding at the planetarium. After the ceremony the guests were shown a star whose light had begun to shine toward the Earth years earlier, when Carol and Eugene first met.

Of course, not many people would want to get married in a planetarium, and most weddings still take place in a traditional church or synagogue.° But today some couples are choosing settings° that are different—very, very different.

Mark Mercer and Janice Pratte loved to ride on roller coasters.° Where were they married? That's right—on a huge roller coaster called the Colossus. As the cars started off, the wedding ceremony began. Speeding down the first hill, the bride and groom° said "I do." Nearing the second turn, they exchanged rings. As they reached the top of the last big hill they kissed, then raced down to the guests waiting below.

Lea Bonham, an elevator operator, and Robert McClure, an elevator repairman, were married in the store elevator where

This couple's roller coaster ride will begin *after* they say "I do."

they had first (met. And Ginger Figueroa and Charles Jones, who both worked for the City Cab Company in Culver City, California, were married in the back seat of a taxi cab.

Ira Kessler and his bride, Sally Hill, didn't even stay on the ground. Married in a hot-air balloon,° they were first pronounced° "husband and wife," and then they went off on their honeymoon.°

Many couples choose these unusual ways to "get hitched"° because it reflects° a shared interest. Some find it is a more

hot-air balloon

named

trip taken by a newly married couple

popular expression for "get married"

shows

Sally prepares to toss
her bouquet from the
hot-air balloon to the
crowd fifty feet below.

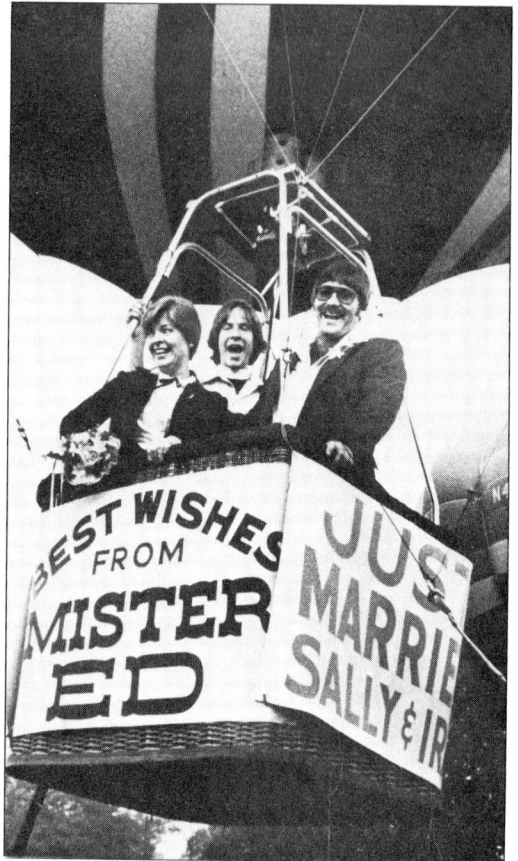

bouquet . . .

not deep / **justice . . .**
officer who conducts
wedding ceremonies

without shoes
enthusiastic . . . people
who enjoy running very
much

personal way to announce their marriage to the world—and
others just want to be original. Vicki and Roger Miller, for example, began their married life in the swimming pool at the
building where they lived. The groom wore a swimsuit, as did
the bride, who also carried a bouquet of flowers.° Standing in
the shallow° end of the pool was the justice of the peace,° bare-
foot° and with his pant legs rolled up.

Bill Stock and his bride Dorothy, both enthusiastic runners,°
were joined together in marriage while jogging on the track at
San Diego State University. The minister ran along with them,
and thirty of the wedding guests, including a seventy-year-old
man, followed behind. At the circus in Oklahoma City, Don and

Alicia Martinez, trapeze artists,° became husband and wife on a trapeze forty feet above the ground. For the honeymoon, however, the location was changed.

trapeze . . .

For a *real* twentieth-century wedding, some couples are using a specially programmed computer. This idea was started by Reinhard Jaenisch, who is a computer specialist and also a minister. For $40, the bride and groom, who can be in any location they want, say "I do" by pushing the computer's "Y" button, for "yes." For $500, the computer will not only speak the words of the minister, but will also play the music of Mendelssohn's Wedding March.

One wedding that will probably not be popular with many other couples was that of John Thompson and Donna Greenberg of Scottsdale, Arizona. John owned a huge garbage° truck which he had built himself, and the two decided to have the wedding there. John and Donna marched down the aisle° between twenty-eight plastic garbage cans and entered the truck, where a justice of the peace was waiting. But no one knows where they went on their honeymoon.

things that people throw away

marched . . .

[627 words]

Adapted from the *Los Angeles Times*

EXERCISES

Questions

1. How many different kinds of weddings were described? What were they?
2. In what order do the following things happen at a wedding: the ring is placed on the bride's finger; the bride is kissed by the groom; the bride and groom say "I do"?
3. Why do people choose different settings for their weddings?
4. Why did Carol and Eugene decide to get married in a planetarium?
5. What was unusual about what Vickie and Roger Miller wore for their wedding?
6. In a computer wedding, how does the minister know when the bride and groom have said "I do"?
7. What does a justice of the peace do at a wedding?
8. Why wouldn't John and Donna's wedding be popular with many other couples?

Dolphins watched this wedding at the city zoo.

Choose the most accurate of the three phrases. ✶   **Vocabulary**

1. To near a turn is to
   a) turn near it.
   b) come close to it.
   c) nearly turn around it.
2. A twentieth-century wedding is one that
   a) is very modern.
   b) began when the couple first met.
   c) is specially programmed.
3. People are "pronounced man and wife"
   a) when they first meet.
   b) when the wedding ceremony begins.
   c) when they "get hitched."
4. Someone who wants to be original
   a) doesn't want to be traditional.
   b) wouldn't get married in a garbage truck.
   c) pays less for a computer wedding.
5. A person who chooses a setting
   a) gets married in a different place.
   b) picks a place.
   c) goes on a honeymoon.
6. If they can be in any location they want, they can
   a) program the computer. ✶
   b) have a traditional wedding by computer.
   c) be far away from the computer.
7. When two people are joined together in marriage, they
   a) carry flowers.
   b) get married.
   c) decide to have a wedding.
8. If something is not unusual, it is
   a) usual.
   b) different.
   c) not traditional.

check dictionary Quiz

early → **earlier** → **earliest**   ✶ **Comparisons**
different → **more different** → **most different**

1. traditional	6. popular	*early earliest*
2. recent	7. shallow	
3. shiny	8. special	*different more different*
4. unusual	9. near	*Quiz. most different*
5. hot *hotter hottest*	10. huge	*Superlative.*

Comparative & Superlative.

Structures

A The husband and wife were happy. →
The husband is happy, as is the wife.
The groom and the bride wore swimsuits. →
The groom wears a swimsuit, as does the bride.

1. The minister and the guests ran along with them.
2. Mark and Janice loved to ride on roller coasters.
3. The balloon and the garbage cans were made of plastic.
4. The doctor and the trapeze artist liked traditional weddings.
5. The church and the synagogue were traditional locations.
6. The flowers and the ring cost a lot of money.
7. The justice of the peace and the parents stood in the pool.
8. The truck and the roller coaster slowed down.

B STUDENT 1: Program the computer, please.
STUDENT 2: **But I *am* programming the computer.**

1. Play the wedding march, please.
2. Place the ring on her finger, please.
3. Show the guests the star, please.
4. Change the location, please.
5. Jog along with them, please.
6. Stand in the shallow end of the pool, please.
7. Stay on the ground, please.
8. March down the aisle, please.

An old fire truck is another unusual place for a wedding.

1. "People who have these unusual weddings really do it to get their pictures in the newspapers. If they really loved each other, they would have a traditional wedding." Do you agree or disagree? Why?
2. Do you think newspapers should write about and show pictures of these weddings? Why or why not?
3. Would you have liked to read the newspaper story about the couple who got married in the garbage truck? What about the ones who got married in the planetarium? Why or why not?
4. Do you think one of these weddings—the garbage truck or the planetarium—was more unusual than the other? Why or why not?

(oral or written)
1. Describe in detail a traditional wedding in your country.
2. Are there unusual settings for weddings in your country? If so, describe them. If not, explain why not.
3. Can you imagine any of the weddings mentioned in the story taking place in your country? Why or why not?

(oral or written)
Describe the kind of wedding you would like to have. If you are already married, describe your wedding. Was it the way you wanted it to be? Why or why not?

14

Same Time, Same Place: A Family Reunion

In the United States, life is changing at an ever faster pace.° People often move from one part of the country to another because of their jobs, or sometimes even without any reason.

But not all Americans lead rootless° lives. Many families are deeply attached to a particular region where they have lived for generations. The Brotzmans are such a family. Here is how the local newspaper reported one of their annual reunions.

Ever since 1913, the descendants of Jacob Brotzman and his wife, Susanna Metzgar Brotzman, have gotten together for an annual reunion. This year, more than eighty-five members of the family met at the Grange Hall in South Auburn, Pennsylvania, on their regular date, the second Saturday in August.

Following a large picnic° dinner that ended with watermelon,° the president, Leonard Brotzman, called the meeting to

Secretary
annual
Picnic

descendants
ancestors

Genealogy
Roots
Root less

Present perfect

rate of speed

moving frequently from place to place

informal meal, often held outdoors
watermelon

A photograph taken at the reunion of the Brotzman family in 1916.

person who writes reports
of meetings

order. The secretary° read reports of other meetings, and then an election of officers was held. Leonard Brotzman, having served three years as president, urged the election of another person. Some people wanted Lee Brotzman, but he asked not to be chosen, since some years ago he had been president for seven years. Instead, Robert Brotzman of Laceyville was elected president.

family history

The Brotzman genealogy° covers the whole family and begins with John Friederich Brotzman, who was born in Germany in 1693 or 1696 and died in 1760. He and his wife, Maria Barbara, came to America on the ship *Bilander Thistle*, which landed at Philadelphia on November 3, 1738.

passed ... died

There was much talk at the reunion about the genealogy and the best and quickest way of getting it printed. (Many of the older family members, who were the people most interested, have already passed away.°) The main difficulty was the amount of money needed: if a hundred or more books were printed, they would cost about eight dollars each. Each person at the reunion was asked to talk to other relatives to find out if they would buy one of the histories if it were printed.

Isaac Brotzman (1842–1863)

Jacob Brotzman (1831–1910)

After the regular meeting, many people looked at the secretary's book, in which the reports of all the reunions are kept. The first reunion was held in the summer of 1913 at the home of Peter and Parnell Warner, a newly built farmhouse in Rush, Pennsylvania. It was a gala affair° with a very large dinner.

gala . . . fancy party

This year, after the reports and readings from the secretary's book, the Misses Barbara and Cheryl Repsher and their sister, Mrs. Clarke Davis of Laceyville, sang for the group, while their grandmother, Mrs. J. D. Brotzman, played the piano. Plenty of ice cream was served to all before the meeting ended.

The next reunion will be held next year on the second Saturday in August at the South Auburn Grange Hall—the same time, same place.

[489 words]

Adapted from *The Wyoming County Courier*

EXERCISES

A *Complete the sentence with a word or expression from the article.*

Vocabulary

1. Your children, grandchildren, and great-grandchildren will be your descendants.
2. Voting to choose leaders is the purpose of an election.
3. A family history is called a genealogy.
4. An informal meal where many people bring food is a picnic.
5. A family with a fixed home in one place is said to have roots in that place.
6. When a ship arrives at a port, we say it landed there.
7. The person who keeps the records of the reunions is called the secretary.
8. An annual meeting is one held every year.

B *In your own words, what is*

1. a family?
2. a reason?
3. a meeting?
4. a relative?
5. a report?
6. a dinner?
7. a region?
8. a sister?

A large picnic dinner was held in the Grange Hall.

C *Fill the blanks with the noun suggested by the verb or adjective in italics.*

1. People lead *rootless* lives. They have no _____ in any one place. *[roots]*
2. Some families are *attached* to a particular region. This _____ is very important to them. *[attachment]*
3. They *elected* a president at the end of the meeting. His _____ came last. *[Election]*
4. Leonard *suggested* that Lee be picked. Leonard's _____ was accepted. *[Suggestion]*
5. Lee asked not to be *chosen*. But he was the Brotzmans' _____ anyway. *[Choice]*
6. The genealogy is finally *complete*. We waited a long time for its _____ *[completion]*
7. The old ship *landed* at Philadelphia. Its _____ was in November. *[landfall]*
8. It's not *difficult* to like ice cream. The _____ is in paying for it. *[difficulty]*

Dates

Repeat aloud.

1. John Friederich Brotzman was probably born in 1696.
2. John Brotzman died in 1760.
3. The ship landed in Philadelphia in 1738.

4. Leonard Brotzman was born in 1898.
5. The fiftieth reunion was held in 1963.
6. The first reunion was held in 1913.
7. Lee Brotzman was president for seven years, from 1949 to 1956.
8. The second Saturday in August, 1913, fell on the ninth.

A The family meets at the Grange Hall. →
For a number of years, **the family has met at the Grange Hall.**

Structures

1. The Brotzmans get together each year. Since 1913, _____.
2. The president calls the meeting to order. Please be quiet, because

   _____.
3. The family chooses a president. The election is over; _____.
4. Most of the relatives buy the genealogy. I am happy to report that

   _____.
5. More relatives come to the reunion. Each year, _____.
6. Each person at the reunion speaks to three relatives about buying
   the books. The secretary announced that _____.
7. We all read the new reports. Once again this year, _____.
8. More Brotzmans visit Germany each year. The book said that

   _____.

That year they talked about the genealogy and how to get it printed.

B Leonard Brotzman served as president. Then he urged the family to elect someone else. →
Leonard Brotzman, having served as president, urged the family to elect someone else.

1. Mrs. Brotzman cut the cake. Then she passed pieces of it around.
2. The committee members finished their business. Then they declared the meeting over.
3. The secretary read all the reports. Then she asked if there were any questions.
4. The family members wrote the genealogy. Then they decided to have it printed.
5. The Repsher sisters sang several songs. Then they said it was time for ice cream.
6. The children ate too much ice cream. Then they cried to be taken home.
7. John Brotzman came to America with his wife. Then he sent for his brother and sister.
8. The family elected Robert Brotzman president. Then they elected Mrs. Davis secretary.

C   The reunion ended after we had all eaten lots of ice cream.   →
    We all ate plenty of ice cream before the reunion ended.

1. The reports were read after we had all drunk lots of ice water.
2. The meeting started after we had all shaken lots of hands.
3. The dinner was served after we had all greeted lots of relatives.
4. The reports were accepted after we had all asked lots of questions.
5. The ice cream was eaten after we had all listened to lots of songs.
6. The cooking began after we had all brought lots of food.
7. The ship landed after we had all spent lots of money.
8. The printer went to work after we had all ordered lots of books.

1. When was the first reunion held?   **Questions**
2. Where was the first reunion held?
3. How many people came to the reunion in this story?
4. Who was elected president?
5. Who is Barbara Repsher's grandmother?
6. What is in the secretary's book?
7. Where was this year's reunion held?
8. On what day are the reunions held?

From what you know and what you have read about people in North   **Personal**
America, which kind of person do you think is more often found there—   **Opinion**
the one who has roots in a particular place or the one who moves around
a lot? Why do you think so?

Prepare a two-minute oral presentation (or one written page) in which   **Report**
you report the main events that took place in your family during the
past year.

Which kind of life—moving from place to place or staying in one place—   **Cross-cultural**
is more usually found in your country? Is that way of life changing? Do   **Topic**
you think it should change? Why or why not?

They Like Being Underground

15

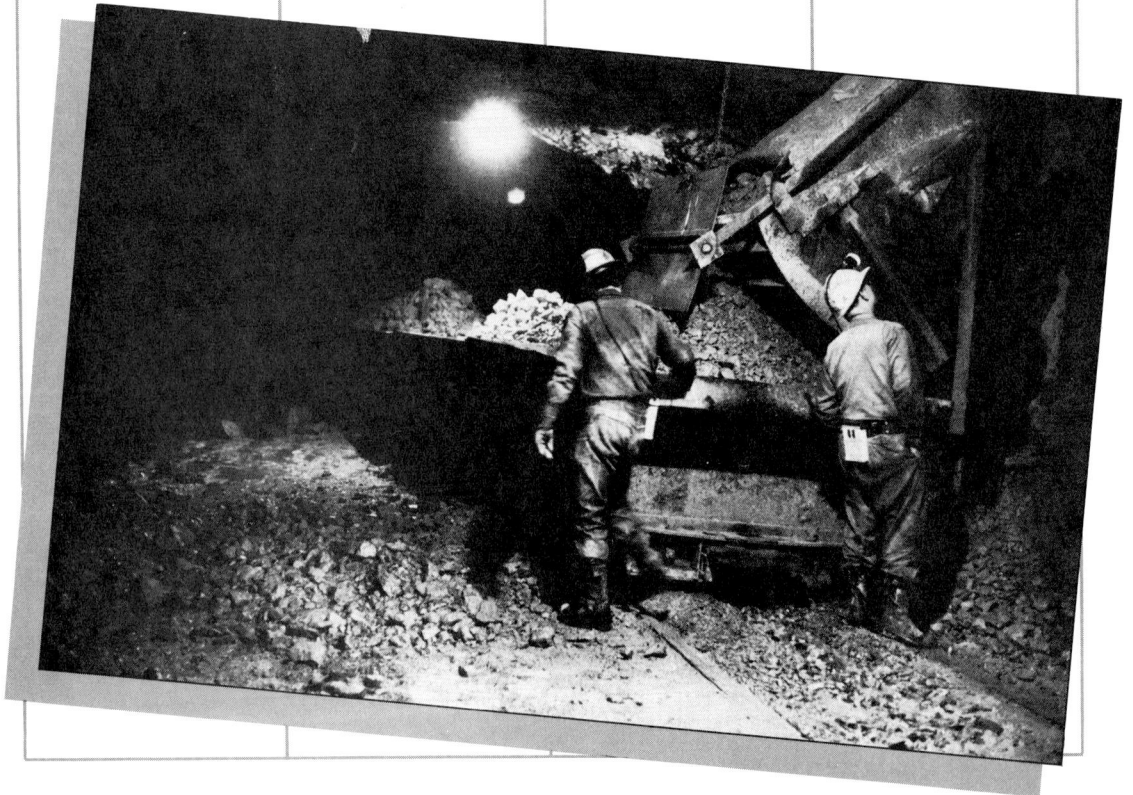

The work may not be fashionable, but for many of the 130 miners at the New Jersey Zinc Company's mine,° there is no other work they would rather do.

deep hole in which people dig out minerals

This is the only mine of this type still operating in New Jersey, a part of the United States not usually thought of as having mines. The miners work nearly two thousand feet under the ground, using modern machinery to produce the richest zinc ore° in the world.

rock that contains minerals

The ore was discovered in 1640, but it contains a mixture of several minerals, and more than 250 years went by before a method was invented to separate the zinc. Since then, the New Jersey mine has been busy and the miners seem to take a special pride in it.

The walls of hard-mineral mines cannot collapse.

coalmine.

Fred Crump, now sixty-six years old, has been a miner most of his life, starting when he was a small boy in a coal mine near his home. "I started mining when I was twelve. I have had jobs above ground from time to time,° but I never liked them as well as working in a mine," he said. Crump, who has worked at the New Jersey mine for seventeen years, compared zinc and coal mines.

from . . . at different times

"Although there is some danger in all mines, coal presents a much greater risk than zinc. Unlike a coal mine, there is no problem with the air quality, and the walls cannot collapse° in a hard-mineral mine like this," he pointed out.

fall down

Crump said he sees great beauty in the mine. "I love the bright colors of the rocks. You can see reds, blues, and purples in the mine walls."

Another person who has worked at mining for a long time is Homer Pennell, who began working in an iron mine almost forty years ago. "Mining may not be the easiest job in the world, but I don't think it's dangerous. Almost all accidents are due to carelessness, and we use lots of safety equipment,"° he said.

safety . . . things used to prevent injuries

Like Crump, Pennell has had opportunities to work above ground, but he prefers mining. "One of the reasons I like to work underground is that the mine is never too hot or too cold. It is especially cool and comfortable to work there in the summer. I can't think of anything I would rather do than work in the mine. I will stay here until I have to retire," said Pennell.

would rather do

Daniel Flores of South America has been working underground for eighteen months and also seems to love mining. "When I arrived in the United States a few years ago, I could not speak a word of English," he recalled.° The twenty-eight-year-old miner said he learned to speak the language the hard way, while working underground. "The first day down in the mine I was scared.° But I had a very good boss,° and in a few hours I lost my fear."

remembered

afraid / someone who directs others at work

Richard Vreeland has worked for five years repairing machinery in the mine. "Obviously,° I could do the same kind of

clearly

Daniel Flores (left) and Doug Francisco are young miners who like their work.

work above ground," he said, "but even though it's dirtier, I just like to work in the mine."

Doug Francisco, a young miner, also loves the job. "The history of the mine means a lot to me. On the walls I can read the names of miners who worked here forty years ago or more. I can imagine how they looked with their old-fashioned° tools and lights." Then the miner's pride in his work came through. "I wonder if they knew that they were producing the richest zinc ore in the world," he said.

something that looks old to us

[618 words]

Adapted from *The Newark Star-Ledger*

EXERCISES

Vocabulary

A *Complete the sentence with a word or expression from the article.*

1. He feels good about his work. He takes _pride_ in it.
2. Zinc is a harder _mineral_ than coal.
3. Are coal mines safer than zinc mines? No, the _risk_ is greater.
4. Special machines _separate_ the zinc from the rest of the ore.
5. Modern machinery is used now. It's not like the old-_fashioned_ equipment used forty years ago.
6. Mine work is not as _easy_ as jogging, but some people like it.
7. The New Jersey mine has _produced_ zinc ore for more than eighty years.
8. "I think of the old miners and try to _imagine_ what they looked like."

B *Choose the most accurate of the three statements.*

1. Bright colors are ones that are
   a) rich with zinc.
   b) easily seen.
   c) not found in coal mines.
2. When you recall something, you

Miners leaving work 2,000 feet under the ground.

a) call it again.
b) talk about it.
c) remember it.

3. Most accidents occur
    a) when people use safety equipment.
    b) when working in coal mines.
    c) when we are careless.

4. A miner who has lost his fear is one who
    a) is not scared.
    b) has a good boss.
    c) works in zinc mines, not coal mines.

5. An opportunity is
    a) a job above ground.
    b) a chance to do something.
    c) found in zinc mines, not coal mines.

6. The hard way to do something is
    a) less easy than the easy way.
    b) less old than the old way.
    c) less dangerous than the dangerous way.

7. To imagine something is to
    a) see it.
    b) form an idea about it.
    c) find out about it.

8. When you take pride in your work, you
    a) have a good opinion of it.
    b) want to stop doing it.
    c) need a new job.

C Fill the blanks with the adverb suggested by the word in italics.

1. Their work isn't *fashionable*, and so they don't dress _____ while doing it.

2. It's a *special* kind of mine, and the equipment is _____ made for it.

3. This is very *rich* ore. The area near the mine is _____ developed.

4. There is *greater* risk in coal mines. But the danger has been _____ lessened.

5. "I love the *bright* colors. Sometimes the mine is _____ lit."

6. It's not the *easiest* job in the world. But it can _____ give you lots of pride.

7. Coal mines are very *dangerous*. But some people like to live _____

8. *Safety* equipment saves many lives. It's always best to work _____

Structures

A They worked with old-fashioned tools. →
I can imagine them working with old-fashioned tools.

1. He opened his eyes wide.
2. He began when he was a small boy.
3. She repaired the special equipment.
4. They produced the world's richest ore.
5. He discovered the mine in 1640.
6. He almost lived underground.
7. She went into the mine last year.
8. They spoke only Spanish.

B I started mining. →
It's time for me to start mining, and there is nothing else I would rather do.

1. He separated the zinc.
2. We worked above ground.
3. He compared zinc and coal mines.
4. They repaired the machinery.
5. She learned a new language.
6. He told us about the history of the mine.
7. They used the safety equipment.
8. She visited the old mine.

C The mine gets cold. → **The mine gets colder.**
The job gets fashionable. → **The job gets more fashionable.**

1. The ground gets cool.
2. The colors get bright.
3. The company gets famous.
4. His eyes get wide.
5. The ore gets rich.
6. The machinery gets specialized.
7. The miners get careless.
8. The work gets dangerous.

Questions

1. Why can't the walls collapse at the New Jersey mine?
2. How old was Fred Crump when he started working there?
3. About when was the zinc-separating method invented?
4. How long has Daniel Flores been working there?
5. When did the old miners write their names on the walls?
6. Why are people surprised to learn that there is a mine in New Jersey?

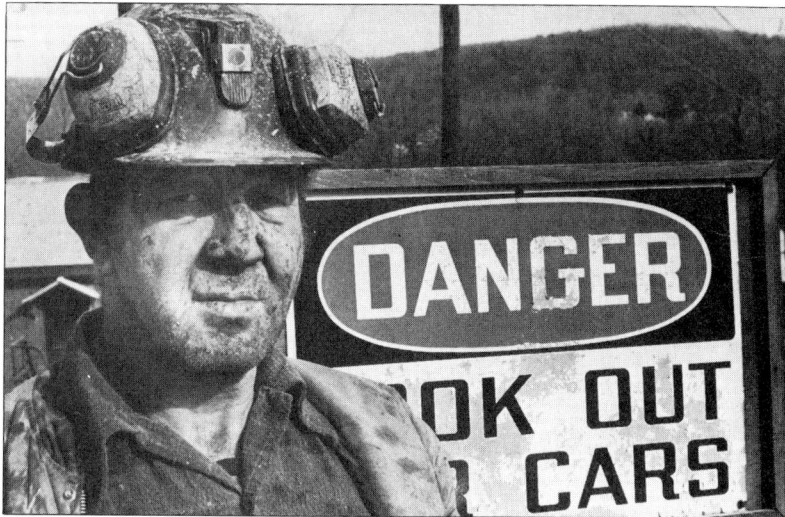

Safety equipment is used in mines to prevent accidents.

7. Why wasn't the ore mined many years ago?
8. Why does Fred Crump think the mine is beautiful?

1. Some people like to work at dangerous jobs. Give as many reasons as you can why someone might like such a job better than a job in a school or office. What kind of job would you like best? Why? Do you think the New Jersey miners really like their jobs as much as they say they do? Why do you think so? Do you know anybody who does dangerous work? Tell the class about this person and what you think about him or her.
2. There used to be laws that said that women could not work in mines or do other kinds of dangerous work. In recent years, many of these laws have been changed, and now women do almost every kind of work. Do you think this change is a good thing? Why or why not? If a woman got a job at the mine in New Jersey, what do you think the other miners would say and do?

Imagination

(for two students at a time)
Pretend that one of you is the boss in a mine, and that the other student is a new worker going down for the first time. Hold a conversation for at least three minutes. The new miner will have lots of questions about the work and the mine, and the boss will explain things and give instructions.

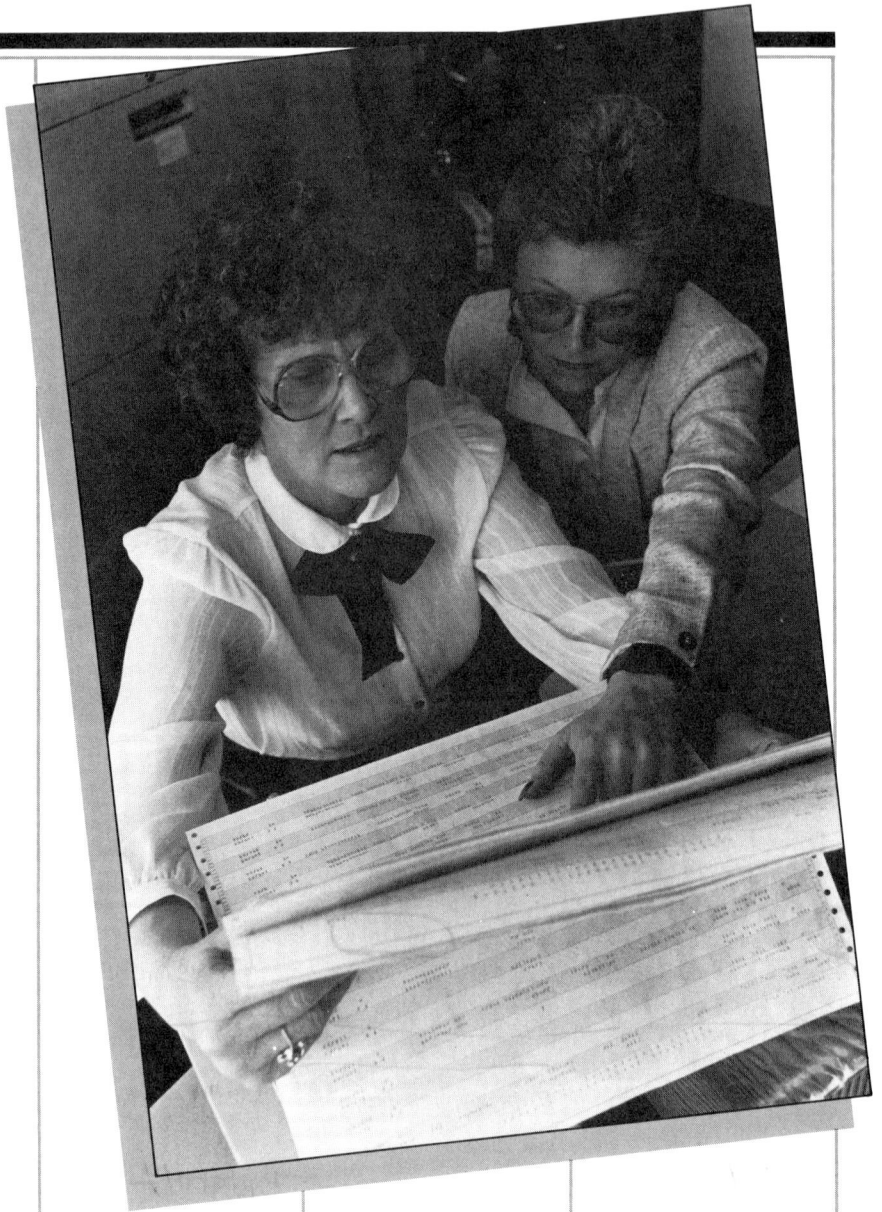

16
Women's Business

More and more enterprising° women are starting and running
their own businesses. Below are some examples of women who
have used their skills to carve a niche° in the business world.

hard-working

carve ... find a place

The Business of Brownies

Row upon row of delicious-looking—and delicious-tasting—
brownies° are lined up behind Laura Katleman, the owner of
"Boston Brownies." While waiting for the lunchtime crowd who
buy so many of her tasty cakes, Ms. Katleman talks about how

small squares of chocolate
cake

Careful research and a
good product helped
Laura Katleman create a
successful business.

she started her business, which has become a success in just three years.

puttered ... liked to cook and bake

"I was never a person who puttered around the kitchen,"° she says. "I started the business because I thought the product would sell. The chocolate-chip-cookie market was at its height. I thought I could have the same success with the brownie—another traditional American food."

As soon as she graduated from college in California, she moved to Boston and set to work on her idea. First, she did some research. To test the public's response to her recipes, she gave away different kinds of brownies in exchange for answers to questions about them. Using the questionnaire findings, she started experimenting with various recipes and eventually came up with thirteen varieties. "I not only wanted to make the best brownies, I wanted to have unusual flavors," she explains. Then she put up signs advertising° the cakes and offering home delivery service. "I was so busy I lost ten pounds, even though I ate many of the brownies myself," she says, recalling that first summer.

making announcements about

Then she was able to rent a space in Quincy Market, a prime° location for small businesses in Boston. She was on her way to success. Since that first summer, she has hired twenty people to work for her and sell her brownies by mail to stores all over the country.

very good

"I feel very lucky to be doing what I'm doing," she says. "When I started, I was intimidated° by experts. People will certainly discourage you when you want to start your own business. But if you have a good product and do your homework,° it's not impossible to succeed. I can't imagine working for someone else now."

made to feel unsure

do ... study

Adjective

Consulting Woman

Elaine Ré sums up in one word what she believes to be the greatest personal reward of running a business: "Confidence."°

She started her international management consulting° busi-

being sure of yourself

giving advice

What kind of business would you like to start?

ness in her apartment, with one student serving as a part-time secretary. Today, six years later, Dr. Ré has a Park Avenue office in New York City and eleven staff members.°

staff ... employees

"I'm thrilled," she says. "It's been very exciting to see the business grow."

After working as a high school and college educator for thirteen years, Dr. Ré entered a doctoral° program in communications at New York University. Then she began her own business as a management consultant. One of her first big jobs, conducting seminars° for a large corporation, attracted the attention of other companies, and her list of clients began to grow. "Conducting seminars combines my love of teaching with what I know about business," she says.

advanced studies

training classes

During the past few years, Elaine Ré and Associates has evolved° into a multi-service organization, offering advice to other businesses all around the world about law, taxes, and how to deal with customers and employees.

developed

"We have seen a growing demand for international negotiating° skills, and no one else seems to be preparing business people who go abroad," she says.

business dealing

As a woman working mostly with male clients, Dr. Ré attributes part of her success to her ability to listen and her desire to teach and help people—qualities she believes many women share. "I think in many ways being a woman in this field has been an advantage, she says. Sometimes it has been a disadvantage, but you fight through those stereotypes° and win acceptance."

general ideas that people have about others

Dr. Ré recommends the experience of running your own business. "It's absolutely a challenge and very rewarding," she says. "And," she adds, "it's a learning experience, whether you make it° or not."

make . . . are successful

She Sews Ideas

Anne Hilliard always enjoyed sewing, and made many of her four chidren's clothes. But when the children grew up Mrs. Hilliard had no one to sew for except herself. Then some of her friends asked her to make more fabric° pen holders like the one she wore on a ribbon around her neck. She began to sell the pen holders, which she called "dePENdables,"* and they were so popular that she began making other items, such as reversible belts° and shopping bags.°

cloth

reversible belt

shopping bag

The business grew. By the end of the first year, she had orders in all fifty states and began to hire sales representatives. Today Anne Hilliard, Inc., has about 2,500 accounts in the United States and also sells its products in Bermuda, England, Japan, and Puerto Rico. To fill the orders, she has twenty-five to thirty local employees, who sew in their homes on a piecework basis.° The company also includes a small staff at her shop. Now that she has a bookkeeper and an accountant° as well as people who do the sewing, Mrs. Hilliard spends much of her time

piecework . . . paid for each item made
bookkeeper . . . people who keep business records

---

* Mrs. Hilliard used the word "dependable" in a special way, to describe someone or something one can be sure of. She found it the perfect way to describe her pen holder (notice the word "pen" in "DePENdable") because when she wore it she could always be sure where her pen was.

designing new products, mostly using traditional American designs.

Mrs. Hilliard particularly enjoys working with her sewing staff. "They take great pride in their work," she says. "If there's a deadline,° they meet it."

a specific time by which work must be finished
specially skilled

Even though her expert° workers are always busy, it is hard for them to keep up with Mrs. Hilliard's new ideas. "Once you get started," she says, "there's no stopping what you can do."

She Deals in Millions

Many people dream of what it would be like to deal with thousands or even millions of dollars. But Beverly Daniel actually does it, every business day. Ms. Daniel is the president of her own commodities brokerage firm° near Detroit, Michigan. It is her responsibility to advise people when to buy and sell in the commodities market, a market where people can earn—or lose— hundreds of thousands of dollars each day.

commodities . . . company that advises on buying and selling goods

Beverly Daniel makes decisions about hundreds of thousands of dollars every day.

customers

Ms. Daniel admits that her business is full of risks, both for herself and for her clients.° Her clients try to make money by buying commodities at a low price and then trying to sell them for a higher price minutes, or months, later. But the prices of commodities (such as grain, metals, food products) change from day to day, even from minute to minute. So many factors influence these price changes—bad weather, insects and plant diseases, war, strikes—that it is difficult to predict° what will happen. That's why many people depend on the advice of a commodities broker such as Ms. Daniel.

tell in advance

Some of Ms. Daniel's customers have made an impressive amount of money by outguessing the market. One of them invested $12,000 in silver, gold, cotton, and sugar and made $6.5 million in less than three years. Another client, trading in silver, went from $1,000 to $9,000 overnight. On the other hand, still another client lost $180,000 within fifteen minutes trading in cocoa. Only Ms. Daniel's quick advice prevented an even larger loss.

This energetic businesswoman learned to be a broker for herself when she invested $6,000 of her own money and watched it grow to $54,000 in just a few months. She began to read more and more about the market and soon, she recalls, "I knew more than my broker and I was hooked."° She went to work for a large brokerage firm. Then, when she felt she knew the business well, she went out on her own. "The only bad thing that could happen was that I could fail," she says. And so, with the firm belief that—given average intelligence, good health, and a will to work hard—anyone can do anything, she plunged into her own business. Now she employs seventy people and has more than eight hundred clients across the nation.

I was . . . I could not stop myself (slang)

Despite the challenge and demands of her job, Ms. Daniel, a divorced mother, takes time each day to spend with her two children. Before starting her business, she served as a judge in Juvenile Court, dealing with the problems of delinquent° and abused° children. Her observations during that time have strongly affected her feelings about being a parent and about

having committed a crime

badly treated, harmed

Each year more and more women begin—and succeed at—running their own businesses.

running a business. "Commodities is a difficult business," she says. "But it is a very small decision to make about what happens to hundreds of dollars compared to making a decision about what happens to a child's life."

[1459 words]

Adapted from *The Christian Science Monitor* and *Ebony*

EXERCISES

Questions

1. In what ways are chocolate chip cookies and brownies similar?
2. Why does Ms. Katleman make thirteen kinds of brownies?
3. How did the "dePENdable" keep Mrs. Hilliard from losing her pens?
4. Why doesn't Mrs. Hilliard do the sewing herself anymore?
5. How can a commodity broker's advice help her clients?
6. How can a questionnaire help to sell cakes?
7. How did Dr. Ré's previous experience help her when she became a consultant?
8. Why do business people need negotiating skills?

Word Families ✗ successful → **successfully**   *Adjectives — write the Adverb*

1. traditional — *traditionally*   6. lucky — *luckily*   11. local — *locally*
2. public — *publicly*   7. certain — *certainly*   12. energetic — *energetically*
3. different — *differently*   8. personal — *personally* 13. expert —
4. eventual — *eventually*   9. international — *internationally* 14. quick — *quickly*
5. busy — *busily*   10. able — *ably*   15. intelligent — *intelligently*

What Happens?

1. when a person *runs a business?*
2. when someone *uses his or her skills?*
3. when *a product sells?*
4. when *a client goes from $1,000 to $9,000 overnight?*
5. when someone *does research?*
6. when *a business grows?*
7. when *an order is filled?*
8. when you *predict* what will happen?

Vocabulary ✗

1. She used the questionnaire *findings.*
   a) losses
   b) answers
   c) questions
2. She offered a *home delivery service.*
   a) She brought the cookies to her customers' homes.
   b) She brought the cookies to her home.
   c) She brought the cookies' customers to her home.
3. She was *on her way to success.*
   a) She was successfully moving.
   b) She was not yet a success.
   c) She was moving her successful business.

4. It's *not impossible to succeed.*
   a) not too possible to succeed
   b) not possible to succeed
   c) possible to succeed

5. The student *served* as a secretary.
   a) gave
   b) worked
   c) typed

6. Many women *share these qualities.*
   a) have the same qualities
   b) teach the qualities to each other
   c) are successful by using these qualities

7. She was *always losing her pen.*
   a) She kept the pen around her neck.
   b) She lost her pen very often.
   c) She lost her pen every time.

8. She *keeps in mind* her year working with children.
   a) trades
   b) invests
   c) remembers

Fill in the correct form of the word in each blank. If you choose a **Word Forms**
verb, check it for correct tense.

1. succeed (v)   success (n)   successful (adj)
   a) Her business was very *successful* she had a lot of customers.
   b) Ms. Katleman *succeed* with her brownie recipe.   *succeeded*   *recipes*
   c) This story tells about the *success* of several businesswomen.

2. confidence (n)   confidential (adj)   confide (v)   *quote.*
   a) The wealthy people had been *CONFIDED* in their broker for years.   *confide*
   b) A broker must keep her customers' business *confidential*
   c) Successful people must have *CONFIDENCE* in themselves.   *confidence*

3. consult (v)   consultation (n)   consultant (n)   *Action*   *Person*
   a) Dr. Ré called in her client for a _____.   *consultation*
   b) Mrs. Hilliard often *consults* her staff for suggestions.
   c) A *consultant* is someone who gives business advice to clients.

4. study (v)   student (n)   studious (adj)
   a) You have to *study* the price of commodities to be successful.
   b) In the cookie business, you must always be a *student* of what   *student*
      people like.   *diversion.*
   c) It's good to be *studious* but it's also good to have fun.   *person*

5. management (n)   managerial (adj)   manage (v)   manager (n)   *Action*
   a) Only one person in each business can be the *manager* .
   b) The *MANAGE* of business is a difficult job.   *manage*
   c) She *manage* her business very successfully for three years.   *managed*
   d) My sister has very good _____ ability.   *management*
      Management

6. able (adj)   ably (adv)   ability (n)
   a) She was a very _able_ worker, and could teach her children.
   b) The _____ to predict commodity prices requires years of experience. *[handwritten: ability]*
   c) She conducts her seminars very _ably_ *[handwritten: ment]*: her clients learn a great deal.

7. tradition (n)   traditional (adj)   traditionally (adv)
   a) _traditional_ cookies are very popular at Christmas. *(Traditional)*
   b) It is an American _tradition_ to eat brownies. *tradition*
   c) Women _traditionally_ never started their own businesses. *traditionally*

8. intelligence (n)   intelligent (adj)   intelligently (adv)
   a) It takes hard work and _____ to be successful. *intelligence*
   b) You'd better invest your money _____, or you might lose it all. *[handwritten: intelligently]*
   c) An _____ person can be successful in business. *(intelligent)*

Structures

A   The consultant has hired a secretary.   →
A secretary has been hired by the consultant.

1. She has rented a space in Quincy Market.
2. Her customers have eaten a lot of cookies.
3. She has taught many international travelers.
4. Judges have helped abused children.
5. Consultants have offered advice to corporations.
6. She has given pen holders to her friends.
7. We have dreamed about millions of dollars.
8. He has sold the commodity at a higher price.

B   She became a consultant. She worked as an educator for thirteen years.   →
Before she could become a consultant, she had to work as an educator for thirteen years.

1. The dePENdables were popular. She practiced on presents for her friends.
2. He called his broker. The price went down.
3. She experimented with various recipes. She sent out a questionnaire.
4. She fought the stereotypes. She got many clients.
5. Mrs. Hilliard employed twenty-five people. The business grew.
6. Her employees made the new products. Mrs. Hilliard designed them.
7. She opened her own business. She studied commodity trading.
8. The experts discouraged her. She rented space in a good location.

C   I advertised the cakes. I offered home delivery. →
    I have been advertising the cakes, and I have offered home delivery.

1. She gave good advice. Her clients made money.
2. She baked many cakes. She lost weight.
3. The children sewed their own clothes. They enjoyed it.
4. She worked hard. She did her homework.
5. They filled the orders. The bookkeeper did the office work.
6. Other people do the sewing. She designed the products.
7. She taught other people. She became successful.
8. We ate too many brownies. We got sick.

---

1. Comment on the last sentence in the article orally or in writing.
2. How do you think the children of the women in these stories are affected by their mothers' spending so much time at work?
3. Which of the four jobs in this story would you most like to do? Which would you least like to do? Why?

Points of View

1. Has the role of women changed in your country in recent years? Could women there have their own businesses, like those in this story?
2. The four women in this story all have their businesses in or near large cities. In your country, are the ideas of people in small towns much different from the ideas of people in large cities?

Cross-cultural Topics

1. What do you think a "dePENdable" looks like? Draw a picture of one, and also describe it in writing, orally, or both.
2. *(for two students at a time)*
Student #1: Describe, in writing or orally, what you think a "dePENdable" looks like.
Student #2: Draw a picture of the "dePENdable" described by Student #1.
Then switch roles, and have Student #1 draw a picture of a "dePENdable" using Student #2's description.

Imagination

The Education of Sarah

17

The chimpanzee may be the animal closest in intelligence° to human beings. How close? Scientists have often tried to develop in chimps the skill that makes man different from all other living things: language. Until now, they have failed; the chimp simply does not have the ability to speak that humans are born with. But psychologist° David Premack succeeded in showing that chimpanzees can "talk" with humans in other ways than by using their voices.

ability to think

scientist who studies the mind

Premack's proof° is Sarah, a female chimp with a vocabulary of more than 120 words. Sarah can understand the meanings of these words, and she can use them to build sentences of her own.

reason for believing something

To teach Sarah, Premack cut shapes out of plastic and attached them to pieces of metal so that Sarah could "write" with them on a magnetic° board. With practice, Sarah learned that a

magnet

Psychologist David Premack taught Sarah how to use language.

fatherly ... pleasure a father feels about the things his child can do

blue triangle° meant an apple, a red square a banana, and so on. In time she learned symbols for each of her four trainers,° plus others for colors and objects such as a pail,° a cup, and a dish. For example, ▨▨ is the symbol for red, and ▨▨ stands for dish.

All this was merely° vocabulary. To teach Sarah grammar, Premack presented a new symbol meaning "on." Sarah learned to understand the purpose of this word by watching him place the symbol for green on the one for blue, the red one on the green one, and so on. One of the first sentences she could understand was a three-symbol statement: ✷ 🍥 ▨▨ ("Green on red"). Before long, Sarah knew how to obey commands in twelve pairs of symbols, and she could do it correctly 80 to 90 percent of the time!

Premack tells with almost fatherly pride° of the day when his student invited her trainer to play a game. The trainer had set up some meaningless sentences—"Red is on banana," "Apple is on green"—merely to test Sarah's understanding of grammar. Suddenly, Sarah began a game. She set out the incomplete

SAMPLE VOCABULARY		
🍶 Sarah	M Mary	X give
▲ apple	pail	dish
red	green	on

SAMPLE SENTENCE
M X ▲ 🍶

These are some of the plastic symbols with which Sarah learned to "write."

YERKISH

WHAT   NAME-OF   THIS

EXPERIMENTER'S QUESTION

M&M   NAME-OF   THIS

LANA'S ANSWER

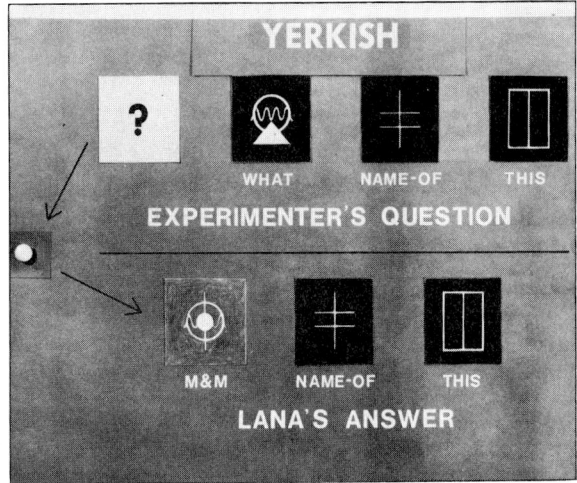

Another chimp named Lana learned to use a computer to communicate.

Vocabulary

sentence "Apple is on . . ." and gave the trainer several possible endings. She considered only one of them, "banana," to be correct. She presented her trainer with various choices until she had taught him the game.

As proof of Sarah's intelligence, Premack tells of an experiment° in which Sarah was given a real apple and asked to choose the symbols for it: red or green, round or square. This she did easily. Then, in place of the apple, she was given its symbol, the blue triangle. Again she was asked to choose other symbols to go with it. Without difficulty, she chose "roundness" and "redness" to go with the blue triangle—proof, writes Premack, "that the chimp thinks of the word not as itself (blue plastic) but as the thing it represents° (red apple)."

test

means

After two years' work with only one chimpanzee, David Premack naturally does not claim anything more than that Sarah has shown intelligent use of language. "This does not mean that she can produce all the functions° of language, or that she can do everything a human can," he writes. "But then," he adds hopefully, "we have only been working with her a short time."

uses

[526 words]

A chimpanzee makes the
sign for toothbrush.

EXERCISES

Vocabulary A *Complete the sentence with a word from the article.*

1. The blue plastic triangle is the *symbol* for an apple.
2. Sarah does not think of it as a blue triangle but as the thing it *represents*
3. The people who teach animals are called their *trainers*
4. If Sarah wants a banana, she must obey Premack's *command*
5. Two similar things that are used together are thought of as a *pair*.
6. If there is more than one way to do something, we have a *choice*.
7. Any special ability—such as the ability to speak a language—is a *skill*.
8. An *experiment* is a way to test an idea.

B *Answer the following in your own words.*

1. What is the difference between *a word as itself* and *the thing it represents?*
2. When a sentence is *meaningless*, what does the sentence mean?
3. What is the difference between a *meaningless* sentence and an *incomplete* one?

4. How can someone *build* a sentence?
5. What is an *understanding* of grammar?
6. What do you do when you *claim* that something is true?
7. Is it easy or hard to do something *without difficulty?*
8. What happens when a person is *invited* to play a game?

C *Choose the most accurate of the three statements.*

1. A chimp is
   a) an experiment.
   b) an ability.
   c) an animal.
2. A square is
   a) four-sided.
   b) long and yellow.
   c) a colored object.
3. Ninety percent of the time is
   a) most of the time.
   b) a short time.
   c) time for more.
4. To be hopeful is to
   a) believe things will never get better.
   b) believe things will get better someday.
   c) believe things will get worse.
5. The ability to speak is
   a) being able to do it.
   b) being taught to do it.
   c) being closest to doing it.
6. A vocabulary is
   a) an ability to speak.
   b) a group of words.
   c) an inborn skill.
7. To consider something is to
   a) work with it.
   b) think about it.
   c) talk to it.
8. To have various choices is to have
   a) less than two.
   b) more than one.
   c) only one.

A STUDENT 1: Can anyone else train Sarah? →
   STUDENT 2: **No, no one else can train her.**

Structures

1. Can anything else be taught to Sarah?
2. Has anyone else done such an experiment?

3. Has anybody else been working with Sarah?
4. Is something given to her for answering correctly?
5. Is something wrong with her mind?
6. Is there anything else you can tell about Sarah?
7. Will someone teach her to talk?
8. Should somebody give her a banana?

B   They ask her to choose the symbols. →
She was asked to choose the symbols.

1. They tell David to stop giving her bananas.
2. They help Sarah to learn the words.
3. They look at her with fatherly pride.
4. They watch him while he moves the new objects.
5. They understand Sarah when she plays the game.
6. They teach her a new language.
7. They give the trainer some green squares.
8. They choose a new chimp to replace Sarah.

Questions

1. What kind of experiment was David Premack trying to do (what was he trying to show)?
2. Why did he choose a chimpanzee for his experiment?
3. About how many words did he succeed in teaching Sarah?
4. What kinds of words did she learn?
5. Did she learn only vocabulary?
6. Can you give an example of one of her "sentences"?
7. Can you tell the story that David Premack was so proud of?
8. Does David Premack claim he has proved that chimps can talk?

Discussion

1. "Teaching a chimpanzee to read and write is a waste of time." Do you agree or disagree, and why?
2. Do you think it would be possible to train any other animals to speak or to use language as Sarah does? Which ones? In what ways could they be taught?

he has Very good equipment
he has a lot equipment

Photograp
Photograper
Photography
Camera
Shoots
(Take)
Cinema (movies)
Cinematographer (Person
(take muving pictures)
cinematography
(skill)
Tripod (stand with 3 feet)
FILMS = movies

lighting = lights
equip ment

18
The Man
Behind the Camera

a - an No
equipment

It took Vilmos Zsigmond almost twenty years to become one of Hollywood's top cinematographers.° A professional cameraman in his native Hungary, Zsigmond came to America in 1956. At first he found it hard to get work doing what he was trained for. But eventually° his talents were recognized and he was asked to work on films such as Close Encounters of the Third Kind, *a science-fiction film that was a great success. In an interview° with* Millimeter *magazine, Zsigmond spoke about some of the problems of his profession.*

person in charge of camera and lighting

after a while

questions and answers

MM: In a number of your films, you've had to deal with bad weather. What difficulties does this create for a cinematographer?

VZ: The weather is always a problem. In Hollywood they used to work in studios° where they could control everything. If you try to shoot° rain the way it is naturally, it doesn't look real on film. Many people think that you just go out into the street and shoot it the way it is, and they think that the new cinematographers like this be-

closed stage for making films
film

The cinematographer adjusts a light while shooting a film.

cause things look more real. But in fact, the lighting is much more difficult outside than on a stage. So we have to work harder to give the audience the feeling they are seeing the real thing. There are more problems but it adds up to more reality, because when they look through a window, they see real trees, real flowers, and real people.

MM: Over the years you have developed a system of shooting with very little equipment. Do you still do that?

VZ: Yes, I like to use the minimum° amount of equipment all the time. I have been using some new lights° that just came out about a year ago. They use very little electricity but they provide as much light as the very big lights used to. And now we use less light because the film itself is much better. Today I think we can use four times less light than we used to need ten years ago.

MM: What about the smaller cameras? Do they help you in your work?

VZ: They help us to get better shots because they fit into places where the older, bigger cameras couldn't go. The smaller the camera, the easier it is. If you have a heavy camera, it takes three people just to lift it onto the tripod.° But you can pick up a small camera, point it, and get your shot. I think it helps a lot in speeding things up.

MM: What kinds of things do you do to prepare for a film before you start?

VZ: I spend a lot of time trying to get to know the director. You know, having discussions, seeing the places we will film, finding out about how the film should look. I want to know what he wants. Many times it is difficult because the director doesn't know yet. I don't want to direct the picture; that's not my job. I want to shoot it the way he wants it to be. If he doesn't have an idea about that, I'll offer some suggestions. I get out color photographs of certain kinds of lighting that would be good for particular scenes. I want to see how he reacts.° That way I find out what he wants.

equipment

as little as possible

lights

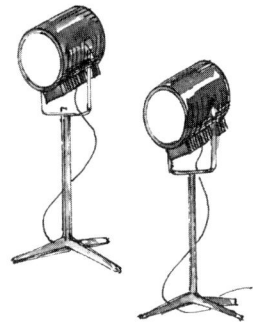

camera

tripod

how ... what he does or thinks about it

Present Participle Used like a noun

Gerund   Gerounds

Sins...

Scenery

MM: In addition to having a good relationship with the director, you've said that the most important thing is having a script° that excites you.

VZ: I have been enthusiastic about almost all of the films I've worked on. I did a couple of pictures where I was excited about the script, but when I started working on it, I was not excited about the director. I want to have fun when I'm shooting a movie. It's hard enough work to begin with, so if you don't enjoy it, what are you doing it for?

[636 words]

Adapted from *Millimeter*

EXERCISES

Vocabulary   **A**   *Complete the sentence with a word from the article.*

1. He likes it very much. He is _____ about it.
2. Can you make the film with so little light? Can you _____ it that way?
3. What did he say about it? How did he _____ to it?
4. I already read the story for that film. It is a _____ I like.
5. He knows how to do that work. He was _____ for it.
6. It provides a lot of light. It is a very good _____.
7. Take as little as possible. Take the _____ amount.
8. It took them a long time, but they got there _____.

B   *Choose the most accurate of the three phrases.*

1. To recognize something is to
   a) find it.
   b) view it.
   c) identify it.
2. To control something is to
   a) direct it.
   b) discover it.
   c) succeed it.
3. Reality is
   a) the way things used to be.
   b) the way things are done.
   c) the way things are.

Vilmos Zsigmond with actor Warren Beatty and director Robert Altman.

4. Your feelings are
   a) how you react.
   b) why you react.
   c) where you react.
5. To prepare is to
   a) get out of.
   b) get going.
   c) get ready.
6. People's relationships are their
   a) large boats.
   b) aunts and uncles.
   c) ways of working together.
7. A discussion is
   a) a talking over.
   b) a talking around.
   c) a talking to.
8. To speed up is to
   a) lift.
   b) go faster.
   c) move above.

Structures

A   The smaller cameras help him in his work. →
     What about the smaller cameras? Do they help him in his work?

1. The new lights use very little electricity.
2. The bad weather creates difficulties for the director.
3. His talents help him keep his job.

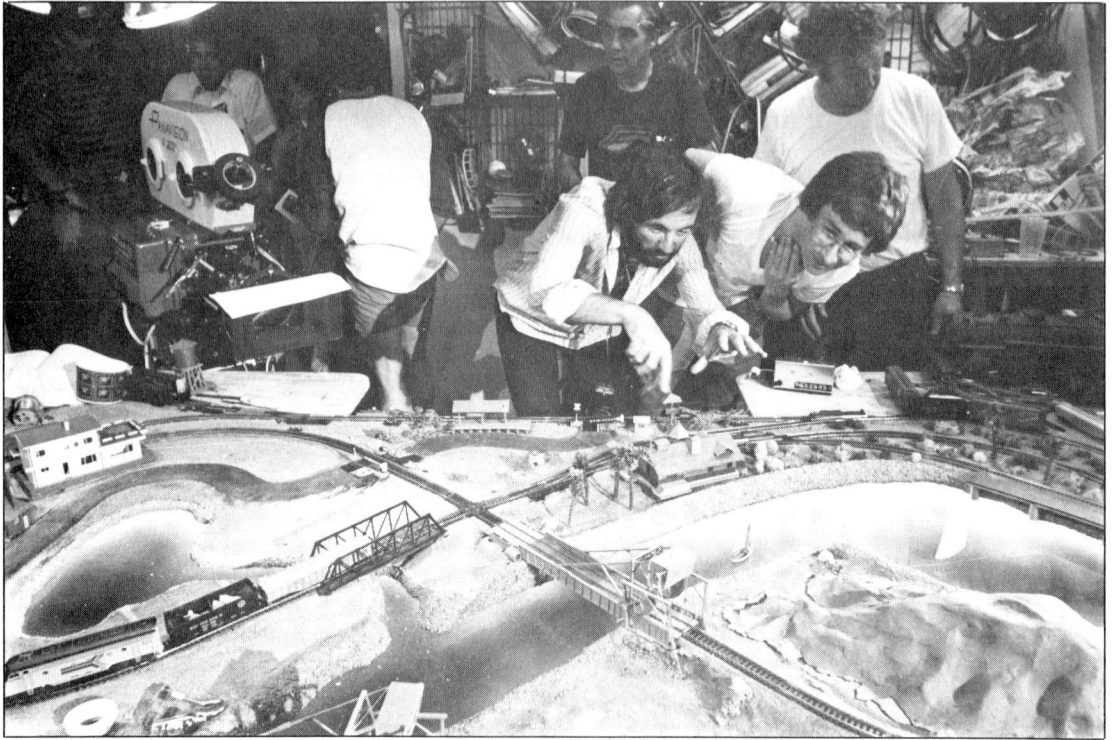

Zsigmond sets up a shot for *Close Encounters of the Third Kind.*

4. The script tells him all he needs to know.
5. These tripods hold the heavy cameras.
6. Science-fiction films have great success.
7. That interviewer knows what she wants to ask.
8. The cameramen enjoy their work.

B The director controlled the writing of the script. →
The writing of the script has been controlled by the director.

1. The cinematographer provided the lighting.
2. Smaller cameras helped the cinematographers.
3. The script doubled the cost of the film.
4. The company completed the film.
5. Millions of people read the story.
6. The actors paid for the meal.
7. Better film dealt with the problem of small amounts of light.
8. The new script excited the man who read it.

C   Don't they pay attention to the script anymore? →
     No, they've stopped paying attention to it.

1.   Don't they use small cameras anymore?
2.   Don't they hire new cinematographers anymore?
3.   Don't they shoot on location anymore?
4.   Don't they go to see his films anymore?
5.   Don't they watch science-fiction films anymore?
6.   Don't they pay a lot of money anymore?
7.   Aren't they working on the script anymore?
8.   Haven't they shot that film yet?

1.   When did Vilmos Zsigmond leave Hungary?   **Questions**
2.   Why were films made in studios?
3.   Why is it harder to shoot films in real places?
4.   Why do they need less light now than they did ten years ago?
5.   How does Zsigmond prepare for a film?
6.   What does he do if the director has not thought about how the film
     should look?
7.   How many people are needed to lift a heavy camera?
8.   Give two reasons why smaller cameras are better to work with.

Is it better to shoot a film in a real place or a studio? If it costs less to   **Points of View**
make a film in a studio, why are many films made outside, in real
places? What if a film being made on the street stops traffic and gets in
people's way?

Write an interview with one of your friends. Ask questions about his or   **Interview**
her work. For example, how long does it take? Is it fun? What changes
have taken place in that kind of work?

19

The Pumpkins
of Half Moon Bay

The little town of Half Moon Bay has become the pumpkin capital° of California. Each year about six thousand tons of this unusual fruit are raised and shipped as far as Hawaii and the east coast of the United States. Yet pumpkins were first grown in the town only in 1934, when a nine-year-old boy planted a few seeds° and grew a crop of his own. Now they are such a big business that Half Moon Bay holds an annual pumpkin festival each fall° that attracts more than 100,000 people. Farmers work all summer to try to grow the biggest pumpkins in the world, and thousands of visitors come to help harvest them.

the most important place

part from which new plants grow

autumn

The festival coincides° with the popular celebration of Halloween, a time for witches° and ghosts,° at the end of October. Children all over the country make scary jack-o'-lanterns° out of

occurs at the same time

ghosts
witches
jack-o'-lanterns

pumpkins by emptying them, carving faces in them, and putting candles inside. The insides of the pumpkins can then be used to bake delicious pies. In fact, it has become a tradition to eat these pies on Thanksgiving, the national holiday in November when Americans celebrate the first harvest of the early settlers. The Indians of the eastern United States had been eating pumpkins long before the first settlers arrived. But the food was not introduced in Europe until the 1500's, when the Spanish explorers brought some back from Mexico—where they were first grown some° eight thousand years ago.

about

Different kinds of pumpkins are better for one thing than for another. The best ones for cooking are the Sweet Sugar and the New England, which grow to weigh about eight pounds. The Tricky Jack is especially good for pies. The best for carving

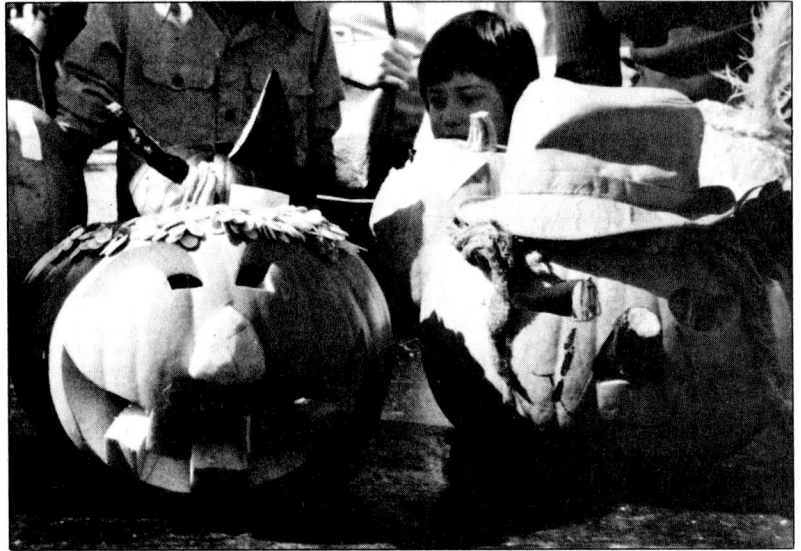

Jack-o'-lanterns are made by carving faces in pumpkins.

are the Big Tom, the Jack-O'-Lantern, and the Big Moon (named for Half Moon Bay), which sometimes weighs twenty pounds or more.*

Grandma's Pumpkin Pie

crushed

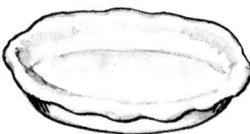

pastry shell

put together / mix smoothly

1½ cups mashed° pumpkin or canned pumpkin

1 cup brown sugar

1 teaspoon cloves

½ teaspoon salt

4 eggs, slightly beaten

1 cup milk

1 unbaked nine-inch pastry shell°

Combine° pumpkin, sugar, cloves, and salt. Blend° in eggs and milk. Pour into unbaked pastry shell. Bake at 350°F for 50 minutes.

[395 words]

Based on *The Pumpkin Book*

* Recently a pumpkin weighing 612 pounds (277 kilograms) won the contest at Half Moon Bay and earned $10,000 for its grower, Norman Gallagher, from the state of Washington.

Pumpkin pie is a
Thanksgiving tradition.

EXERCISES

A *Complete the sentence with a word or expression from the article.*   **Vocabulary**

1. In order to grow a crop, a farmer must <u>to Plant</u> seeds.
2. Something that is done over and over again becomes a <u>Tradition</u>
3. If it is done every year, we can also say that it is <u>annualy</u>
4. If two things take place at the same time, they <u>Coincides</u>
5. The explorers <u>brough</u> the pumpkin to Europe.
6. The Big Moon was <u>named For</u> Half Moon Bay.
7. To combine is to put <u>together</u>
8. In the fall, thousands of people come to help <u>harvest</u> the pumpkins.

B *Choose the most accurate of the three words or phrases.*

1. A pumpkin is a
    a) festival.
    b) pie.
    c) <u>fruit.</u>
2. Seeds are usually planted
    a) at harvest time.
    b) <u>in the ground.</u>
    c) in Mexico.
3. Thanksgiving is a
    a) <u>celebration.</u>
    b) settlement.
    c) harvesting.
4. The first pumpkins were grown there some forty years ago.
    a) <u>About forty years ago, pumpkins were first grown there.</u>
    b) Some pumpkins were grown there first.
    c) Forty years ago pumpkins were grown about there.

To Plaut
Tradition
annualy
Coincides
brought
named For

harvest

5. Pumpkins spread around the world.
   a) They became big business.
   b) They went to Europe.
   c) They were grown everywhere.
6. Fall is a
   a) season.
   b) holiday.
   c) festival.
7. To carve a face in a pumpkin is to
   a) smile at it.
   b) cut holes in it.
   c) place a candle inside it.
8. Halfway is
   a) at the end of something.
   b) at the middle of something.
   c) in the name of something.

Some of the biggest pumpkins in the world grow in Half Moon bay.

The pumpkin has been around a long time—at least 8,000 years.

a Scarecrow

C *Fill in the blanks with the nouns suggested by the adjectives in italics.*

1. Halloween used to be very *popular*. Now it is losing some of its popularity

2. The freshly baked pie smelled very *pleasant*. It was an even greater pleasure to eat it.

3. Grandma's *celebrated* pumpkin pie is worthy of any Celebration.

4. It is a *national* holiday because it is very important to the Nation.

5. Thanksgiving is a *festive* occasion. It is one of our best Festivities.

6. The *combined* effect of the pies and cakes and fruits and vegetables was to make us all gain weight. It was a powerful combination.

7. *Different* kinds of pumpkins are better for some things than for others. There is definitely a difference.

8. The Spanish *explored* Mexico and later *settled* there. They were both explorers and Settlers.

Celebrate
Present Participle
Past Participle
amuse as Adjetives
Breaking News

Present Participle
as a noun =
Geround

A Each holiday has a special name. →
The different holidays are given special names.

Structures

1. Each jack-o'-lantern has a special face.
2. Each baker has a special kitchen.
3. Each season has a special meaning.

4. Each pie has a special taste.
5. Each festival has a special day.
6. Each farmer has special seeds.
7. Each ghost has a special story.
8. Each child has a special pumpkin.

B   How slowly pumpkins grow! →
One thing that makes pumpkins different is that they grow so slowly.

1. How many pumpkins Half Moon Bay has!
2. How big their festival is!
3. How much this pumpkin weighs!
4. How good that pie tastes!
5. How popular the celebration is!
6. How easy it is to carve jack-o'-lantern faces!
7. How much fun it is to write these exercises!
8. How hard the farmers work to grow large pumpkins!

C   Both pumpkins and other fruits grow slowly. →
Pumpkins grow slowly, as do other fruits.

1. Both the children and the farmers like the festival.
2. Both the settlers and the Indians liked to eat them.
3. Both the witches and the ghosts celebrated.
4. Both the Sweet Sugar and the Big Tom weighed ten pounds.
5. Both October and November are months.
6. Both the women and the men baked tasty pies.
7. Both 1934 and 1970 were good years for the pumpkin in California.
8. Both Mexico and the United States grow fruit.

Questions

1. When were pumpkins first raised in Half Moon Bay?
2. What holiday takes place in November?
3. What does that holiday celebrate?
4. Which pumpkins are among the best for carving?
5. How many pumpkins are grown in Half Moon Bay?
6. How much sugar do you use to make a pumpkin pie?
7. Where were pumpkins first grown?
8. How old is the pumpkin?
9. How much did Mr. Gallagher's prize-winning pumpkin weigh?

1. What are the advantages and disadvantages of growing only one major crop in a particular place?
2. Why do you think some people say "as American as pumpkin pie"?
3. How do you think harvest festivals developed?

Are special festivals held in your country to celebrate the harvest or certain foods? Tell the class about them. Do you have a national dish or some food that is very popular in your country? How is it made?

The Artists' Retreat

20

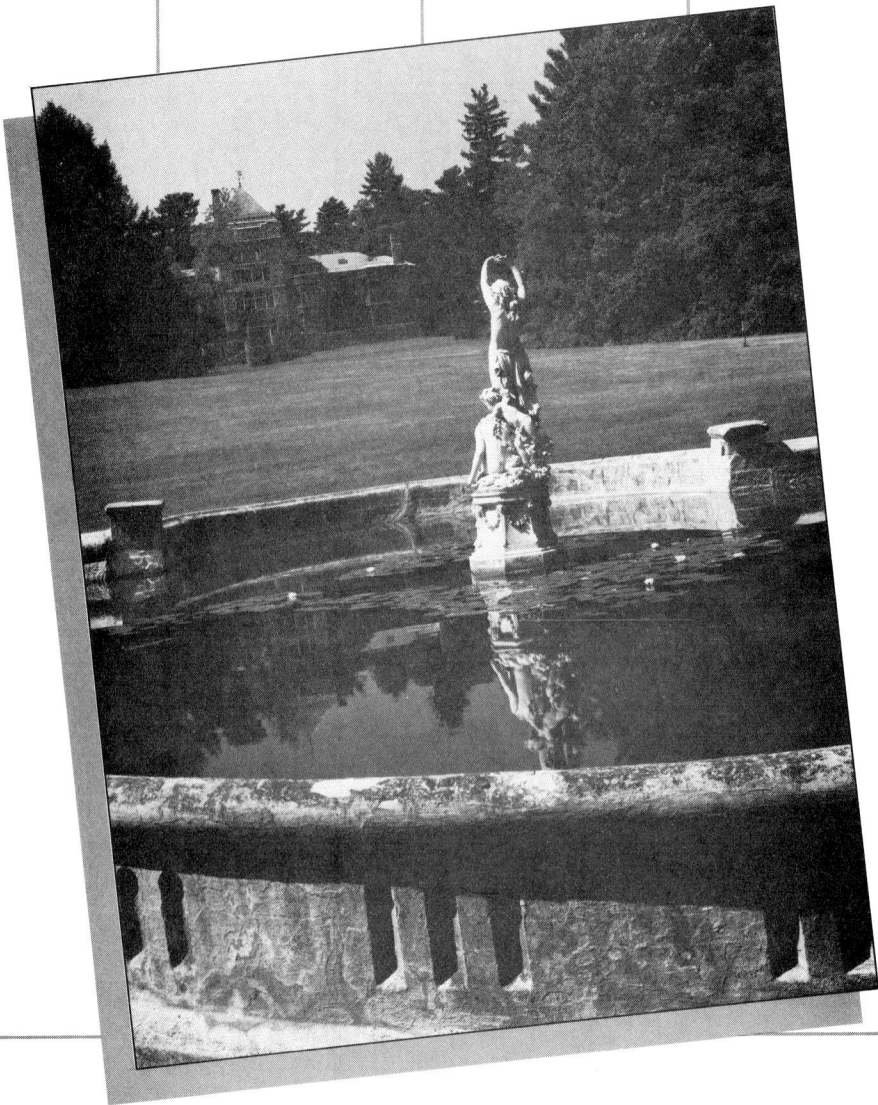

Imagine a beautiful, quiet place in the country, surrounded by trees, small lakes, and streams. Imagine no phone calls or television or interruptions of any kind, helpful people to do one's cooking and cleaning, and nothing to do all day but write or paint or compose music.

The idea of such a place, where writers, musicians, and other artists can do their work without having to worry about making a living, seems like a dream. Yet such places do exist—special "colonies" where artists of all kinds can live and create in complete freedom, away from the outside world.

The first of these was the MacDowell Colony, begun in 1910 in Peterborough, New Hampshire. Other well-known colonies are Yaddo and the Millay Colony in New York State, and the Virginia Center for the Performing Arts.

At Yaddo, near Saratoga Springs, over two thousand writers, painters, sculptors,° photographers, and composers° have come together since 1926, and have completed some of their most important creative work there. In over half a century the daily routine° has changed very little. A typical day still begins with an early group breakfast. Afterward, guests (as visiting writers and artists have always been called) pick up their lunches and go off to work in private studios.

The only rules at Yaddo are there to ensure° each guest's privacy. Quiet hours extend from 9 A.M. to 4 P.M. and no guest may be disturbed during this time without a direct invitation. A telephone call to a guest at the Yaddo office (there are no phones in rooms or studios) results in a message left in the dining room. It has been suggested that not only the lack° of interruptions but the lack of the *threat* of them makes Yaddo perfect for creative work.

Most of the artists stay for a month or six weeks and find that they can produce more during this time than in the same time at home. Curtis Harnack, the director of Yaddo, says that people are amazed by what they can accomplish there. "Sometimes they double the amount of work they normally get done. It's the concentrated° uninterrupted time you get here. It allows

sculptor

people who write music

the system of doing things

make sure of

absence

centered on one thing

At an artist's colony, this painter can work all day without interruptions.

you to get deeper into your work, and go farther. All the other supports—the fact that you don't have to shop, you don't have to clean, nobody can reach you while you work—all of that is time protection."

Says Sue Standing, whose book of poetry was partially written at Yaddo, "Being there was the first time in my life when I had a whole month just to write. Without that long period of time, I don't think I could have done it."

Such statements about the great importance of uninterrupted time are borne out° by the long list of books that have been written at Yaddo. The names on the books in the Yaddo Authors' Library read like a "who's who" of modern American writers: James Baldwin, Saul Bellow, Truman Capote, Malcolm Cowley, Langston Hughes, Dorothy Parker, Sylvia Plath, Mario Puzo, Lionel Trilling, Eudora Welty, William Carlos Williams. Yaddo has also been visited by many distinguished° visual artists, including painter Philip Guston, sculptor George Rickey, and photographer Henri Cartier-Bresson. Aaron Copland and

borne ... shown to be true

outstanding

Leonard Bernstein are among the many composers who have worked there.

He was death

Indeed, it is no wonder that the late John Cheever, whose novel *Falconer* was begun and finished at Yaddo, once said, "The 40 or so acres on which the principal buildings of Yaddo stand have seen more distinguished activity in the arts than any other piece of ground in the English-speaking community or perhaps in the entire world."

Passive Voice

The time is there for the artists to use, but not all the artists are able to use it properly. Jacqueline Berke recently spent a month at the MacDowell Colony. She said she was so happy being there that, on her first day, she thought about all the time she would have in which to write. But she spent so much time thinking that she had no time to write. The same thing happened on the second day, and again on the third. Finally, on the fourth day, she decided to do something about her problem, so she walked to a nearby store and bought paper and pencils and pens. Still no writing. On day five, she arranged all her supplies° neatly

°things needed for one's work

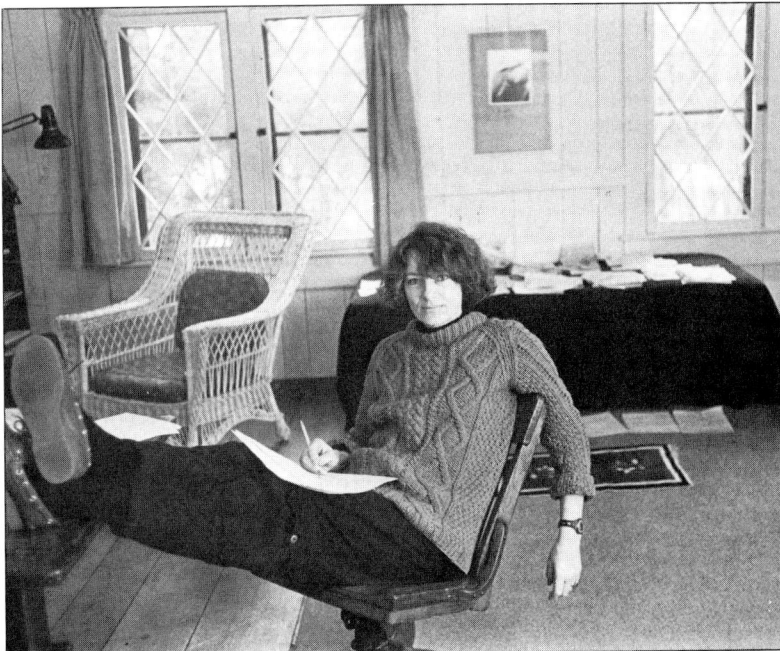

Many famous authors have worked in the studios at Yaddo.

on her desk. Day six, she stayed late at breakfast and helped the workers clean up. Day seven, she moved from her chair in front of the typewriter to a more comfortable couch—and fell asleep.

Finally, she began to write. Her first work was a story called "Wasting° Time at a Writer's Colony."

making poor use of

Of course, most of the visitors use their time wisely and, over the years, thousands of fine writers and artists have done *Present perfect* some of their best work at one of these colonies. As writer Rebecca Rass said recently, "I always imagined there would be a place like this somewhere. This place *is* a dream."

[825 words]

Adapted from *U.S. Air* and *Shoptalk*

EXERCISES

Fill-ins

Practice Present Participle ✗

Read each sentence aloud, filling in the blank with an -ing word based on the article.

She is not doing her work; she is **wasting** time.

1. Someone else does the _cooking_ and _cleaning_ at Yaddo.
2. She spent so much time _thinking_ about it that she never began to write.
3. People _calling_ on the telephone might disturb the artists.
4. The writers write books while the musicians are _composing_ music.
5. That photographer is _taking_ my picture.
6. She is just _moving_ back and forth from the chair to the couch.
7. It is _amazing_ how much work can be done at a writers' colony.
8. He is near the end of his novel. He is _finishing_ it. *finishing*

Vocabulary

A *What is*

1. an artists' colony?
2. a novelist?
3. a creative work?
4. an interruption?
5. the "outside world"?
6. a group breakfast?
7. a modern writer?
8. a visual artist?

Artists might meet here after a day's work.

B *Fill in the blanks with* nouns *suggested by the verbs or adjectives in italics.*

[handwritten: composures composer (n) / compositor (n) / composure (n)]

1. He has been *composing* for years, but there are still other _____ to write.
2. *Dreaming* about something won't make the ___dream___ come true. *[handwritten: dream]*
3. If you *accomplish* it, that would be a great __accomplishment__ *[handwritten: accomplishment]*
4. It has been *suggested* that the artists need quiet. I think that is a good __suggestion__. *[handwritten: suggestion]*
5. Don't *disturb* the writer. No __disturbance__ is allowed. *[handwritten: disturbance]*
6. It is very *important* to have enough time. That is of great __importance.__ *[handwritten: importance.]*
7. She *wasted* all that time. What a _____! *[handwritten: waste Waste wastage waster wastrel]*
8. Phone calls kept *interrupting* me. I wanted to work without __Interruption.__ *[handwritten: Interruption.]*

Questions

1. Why do artists need privacy?
2. What is the difference between a musician and a visual artist?
3. What is "time protection"?

4. If an artist at Yaddo wanted to talk on the telephone at 3 P.M., could he do so? How?
5. How can artists get "deeper" into their work?
6. When was Yaddo opened? How large is it?
7. What problem did Jacqueline Berke decide to do something about on the fourth day?
8. Where do the artists eat lunch at Yaddo?

Structures

A   She remembers when she lived at Yaddo. →
She remembers living at Yaddo.

1. She remembers when she cleaned her own house.
2. She remembers when she came to the artists' colony.
3. She remembers when she bought the pencils.
4. She remembers when she wasted all that time.
5. She remembers when she disturbed the sculptor.
6. She remembers when she picked up her lunch.
7. She remembers when she went off to her studio.
8. She remembers when she completed her work.

A lunch basket waits on this artist's doorstep.

B   STUDENT 1: Joe, did you finish that novel yet?
STUDENT 2: **Oh, yes, I finished it two weeks ago.**
STUDENT 1: I didn't hear you. What did you say?
STUDENT 2: **I said I already finished it.**

1. Sue, did you read that book of poetry yet?
2. Curtis, did they do their work yet?
3. John, did you come to the end of your novel yet?
4. Jacqueline, did you start writing your story yet?
5. Leonard, did the visitor call you yet?
6. Rebecca, did Dorothy arrive at Yaddo yet?
7. Mr. MacDowell, did they open the retreat yet?
8. Edna, did he show you the list yet?

C   They do their work there. →
They can do their work there now, but they couldn't a year ago.
They can't do their work there now, but they could a year ago.

1. They complete their creative work.
2. They enjoy complete freedom.
3. They spend all their time dreaming.
4. They have a group breakfast.
5. They visit the artists' colony.
6. They begin at 9 A.M.
7. They are free from home computers.
8. They stay for a month.

Points of View

1. In what ways would the world be worse (or better) if there were no such places as Yaddo?
2. How do you like to do your own work? Do you like to work in private and quiet, or do you like to work under a lot of pressure? If you could work at Yaddo, do you think you would do a lot of work, or waste a lot of time? Why? Do you think there is anything wrong with people who waste time? Why or why not?
3. "Artists should not be treated differently from anyone else. Other people have to live with interruptions, yet we expect them to do good work. There is no reason to make special arrangements for artists." Do you agree or disagree with this statement? Give reasons.

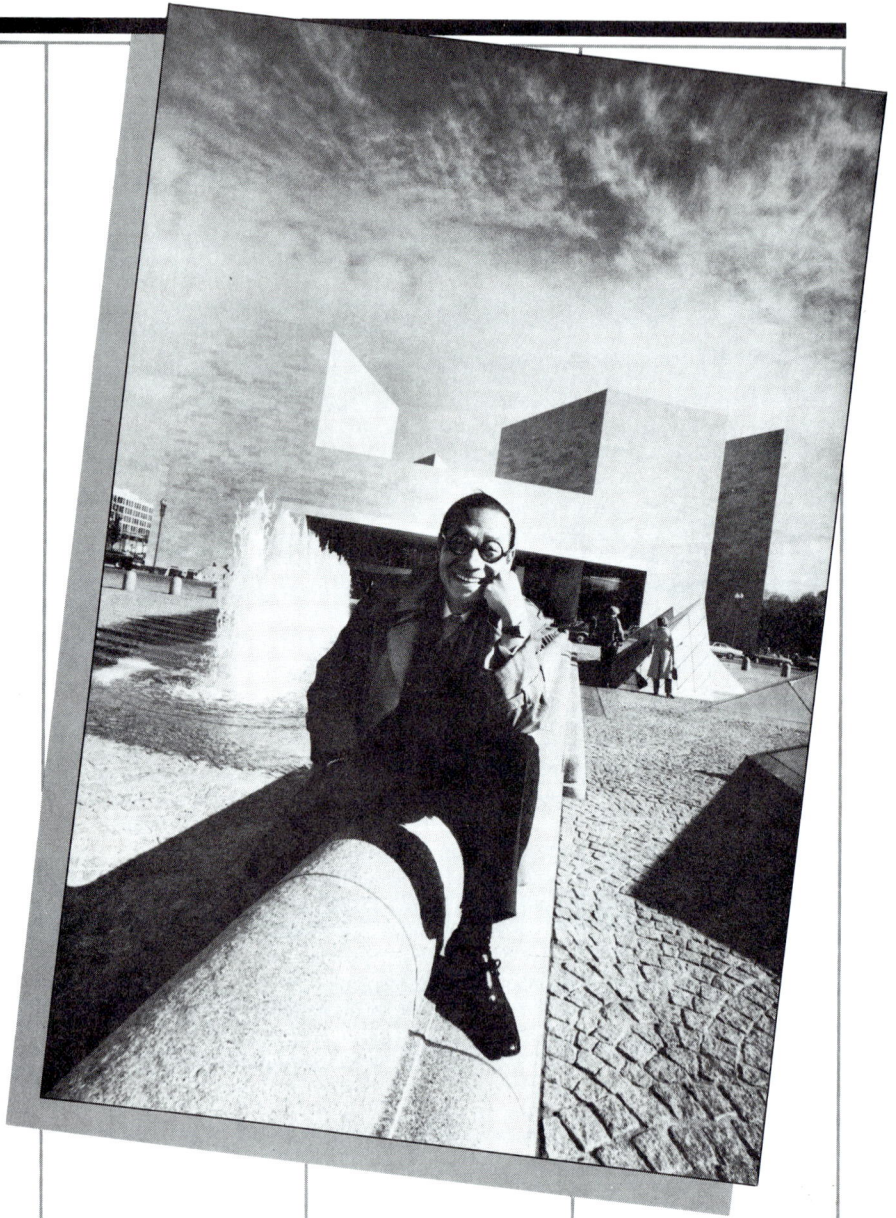

21
I. M. Pei

present prog.

I. M. Pei is pacing his living room floor, talking about architecture.° "It is not just an idea, but the way in which that idea is done, that is important. This is what I mean by the 'architecture of ideas.' I worry that ideas and the practice of architecture as a profession, as a business, do not come together often enough." He pauses, then adds: "Maybe my early training set me back. Maybe it made me too practical."°

That is an unexpected comment from a man like Pei, who runs a business that employs 160 people and has important clients all over the world. I. M. Pei questioning the value of being practical might seem like a bank doubting the value of money. Yet his company, I. M. Pei & Partners,° is more than just a business that designs buildings. It has always tried to bring together beauty and art with professional business sense, and today it is probably the leader among American architectural companies that do very well both artistically and commercially. It is hard enough to become well known either as an artistic or as a business success in architecture: to do so in both areas is remarkable.

I. M. Pei, a leader in his field for more than twenty years, seems to get better and busier as the years go by. One reason for his success is his personality, for he is well known as a kind and thoughtful person. But it is also because of the seriousness of his work. He believes in improving on and developing from styles and designs that have been used before, not in newness° for its own sake. Companies hire him because they believe that his designs are strong and modern without being shocking.

Pei's style is based on geometric forms, like most of the architecture of modern times. But he has continued to use these forms while other important architects have begun to change their styles, making use of the forms of architecture from other countries and other periods in history.

Ieoh Ming Pei was born in China in 1917, but he calls himself "an American architect—absolutely."° He came to the United States in 1935 to study architecture, and remained here because of the war. In the late 1940s he got a very good job and

the design of buildings

concerned mainly with results

people who own a company

New things

completely

This part of the National Gallery in Washington, D.C., was designed by I. M. Pei.

decided to become an American citizen. He has lived in New York since then, but he has never forgotten the land of his childhood.

In 1978 Pei was invited to design a hotel in China. It was a very difficult thing for him to do because as he said at the time, "there seem to be only two choices—either to copy the old Chinese style with red columns and golden roofs or to build modern Western buildings. I do not think either of these is right. There has to be a third way."

Pei's "third way" included traditional Chinese design, as well as garden courtyards. He used many Chinese materials and forms, but gave the hotel a flat roof instead of a traditional curved one because it was safer and less expensive. The hotel, named

Fragrant Hills, opened in 1982. It is state-owned and entirely managed and run by Chinese.

In New York City, I. M. Pei & Partners will build a convention center° that will be much bigger than the hotel in Peking, and in some ways much simpler. In fact, the biggest problem is that the center may look too much like a large box. Therefore they are working to create a number of public areas within the one huge space. These will be used for other things even when there are no special meetings or shows, and will make the building itself into a tourist attraction.

It is possible that Pei's way of working may soon change, becoming more like one or the other of the two major modern directions. He might decide to make more use of the styles and ideas of the architecture of older cultures (as he did with his

convention . . . large
building for meetings and
shows

In 1978 Pei was invited
to design a hotel in
China.

Pei's "third way" puts together traditional and modern styles.

hotel in China) or he might decide to treat his buildings even more artistically (as he did the Kennedy Library in Boston). But it does not seem likely that Pei's work will move strongly in either direction. He believes his work gives his clients what they want and he tries to make his buildings fit the jobs they are supposed to do.

[795 words]

Adapted from *The New York Times Sunday Magazine*

EXERCISES

Vocabulary ✗ A *Complete the sentence with a word or expression from the article.*

1. If architects don't please their _clients_, they aren't likely to get more work.
2. Pei is a leader in the _field_ of architecture. *Field*
3. If you want results, you'd better be _practical_ about it.
4. They own the company together; they are _partners_
5. The two styles differ only in one important _design_
6. The place where he grew up is the land of his _childhood_
7. This building was built in another _period_ of history. *Period*
8. I don't believe it is worth it. I _doubt_ the value of it. *question*

Third way
Architecture ✗5.

Adjectives: Describes Nouns

ends in:

Word ends
I ble ⟩ Adjectives
able ⟩

Word ends
Ful = Adjective

Nale :
Adjective

B *Fill in the blank in each of the following sentences with the noun suggested by the adjective in italics.*

1. They had great Admiration _____ for the young architect's work, which was *admirable*.
2. She came under the influence _____ of the old style and based her designs on it; that's how *influential* it was.
3. They had doubt _____ about the value of the idea. It was *doubtful*.
4. The *Chinese* style is found largely in China _____.
5. It was certainly *remarkable* that no one had made a remark _____ about it.
6. Her *commercial* dealings made her famous in the world of Commerce _____
7. Others might find it *difficult*, but Pei had no difficulty _____ in deciding to build a hotel in China.
8. *Artistic* talents can be very useful to an Artist _____

C *Choose the most accurate of the three words or phrases.* ✱

1. A comment is something someone
   a) builds.
   b) says.
   c) has.
2. To be successful in business is to
   a) build lots of buildings.
   b) make lots of money.
   c) use lots of space.
3. A practical hotel building is one that is very
   a) small.
   b) simple.
   c) useful.
4. Something that is absolutely true is true
   a) without any doubt.
   b) in a practical way.
   c) in some aspects.
5. A thoughtful person is one who
   a) is full of thoughts.
   b) is careful to think of other people. ✗
   c) often thinks.
6. If you copy something, you
   a) make something just like it.
   b) build another thing.
   c) use it for something else.
7. If something looks too much like something else,
   a) we don't look at it too much.
   b) we think they look the same.
   c) we look at them the same way.

Pei's style is based on geometric forms.

8. Newness for its own sake is dangerous because
   a) life is too short.
   b) oldness is always better.
   c) it will probably not be practical enough.

Structures A I like artists who use old styles. →
The kind of artist I admire most is one who uses old styles.

1. I like architects who use modern ideas.
2. I like houses that have large rooms.
3. I like buildings that are successful artistically.
4. I like paintings that never look old.
5. I like hotels that are small and comfortable.
6. I like companies that use professional artists.

7. I like people who are kind and thoughtful.
8. I like clients who know what they like.

B   Do banks doubt the importance of money?   →
It is hard to believe that a bank would doubt the importance of money!

1. Do architects build small rooms?
2. Do businessmen prefer beauty to money?
3. Do designers copy old styles?
4. Do convention centers hold only twenty people?
5. Does the world of ideas concern itself with business?
6. Did the Chinese build Western buildings?
7. Does his personality make people angry at him?
8. Does their hotel look like a box?

Questions

1. Where will Pei build a giant convention center?
2. How does Pei's early training show in his buildings?
3. How does I. M. Pei & Partners make money?
4. How old is I. M. Pei this year?
5. When did I. M. Pei come to the United States?
6. How long has he been a leader in his field?
7. Why do companies hire him to design buildings for them?
8. How does his hotel in China differ from traditional Chinese architecture?

Discussion

1. "All architecture is basically either for people to live in or to protect the things they value." Do you agree with this statement? If not, what other basic functions do you think architecture has?
2. "What difference does it make what a building looks like from the outside?" How would you answer this question?
3. If you saw the Peking hotel and the New York convention center and did not know who the architect was, could you tell they were designed by the same person? If so, how? If not, why not?

Cross-cultural Topic

What is characteristic about the architecture in your country that makes it different from that of other countries? What do you think are the reasons for those differences? Could those characteristics be used in the United States?

It's Written in the Stars

22

For thousands of years, people have believed that the position of the stars affects our lives. This may or may not be true, but there is no doubt that astrology° itself does affect our lives. Most newspapers in the United States print horoscopes,° and about forty million people read them every day. Many young people plan to marry at a time when their horoscopes will be favorable, while others decide not to marry because their signs are not harmonious.° Some companies have hired astrologers to advise them, and one well-known businessman prefers to do his most important work at 3:00 A.M. because he was told that it is his most favorable hour. But even skeptics° can't be sure that they are not affected by what the stars say. How do you know, for example, that your employer, your best friend, or perhaps even your husband or wife is not secretly following the directions of a horoscope?

the study of how the stars affect people's lives

what the stars say will happen

signs . . . they do not get along well with another astrological type

nonbelievers

Aries   March 21 to April 20

Persons born under the sign of the ram tend to be enthusiastic and are not afraid of difficult situations. They are natural leaders who like to bring about changes in the world, and they may do so as generals or politicians. Often impulsive,° they welcome hard work and get things done without wasting time, but they are sometimes thought of as egotistical° because of this.

Harmonious signs: Sagittarius and Leo.

acting without thinking

thinking mostly of themselves

Taurus   April 21 to May 21

The sign of the bull is a fitting one for Taureans, who are strong and known for working hard. They understand the importance of order and try to establish a system for their lives. Many are

not willing to change

sense . . . ability to see the funny side of things

found in government work. Although sometimes stubborn,° Taureans are not always serious, and usually have a good sense of humor.°

Harmonious signs: Capricorn, Virgo, and Cancer.

Twins

Gemini   May 22 to June 21

Clever and full of energy, Geminis are experts at dealing with other people. Because of their ability to use their minds well and their desire to express themselves, they make good inventors, scientists, and magicians.° They are excited by the new and the different, and need a lot of variety in both their personal and professional lives.

Harmonious signs: Aquarius and Libra.

magician

Cancer   June 22 to July 22

respond easily to feelings

Those born under the sign of Cancer are very sensitive,° so they laugh and cry easily. They change their minds often, but when they decide that they really want something, they don't let go of° that desire. Cancers love their homes and families, and are interested in history and ancient objects. They have strong imaginations, so that they make good teachers, public speakers, and writers.

don't . . . keep

Harmonious signs: Pisces, Scorpio, and Taurus.

Leo   July 23 to August 23

The lion is the sign of those who are born to command. They are proud people who may appear to be self-concerned and egotistical, but they are frequently generous and understanding.

It is not surprising to find that they are often politicians or the directors of large companies.

Harmonious signs: Sagittarius and Aries.

Virgo   **August 24 to September 23**

Virgos are clear-thinking, careful, and hard-working. Although they have the ability to organize,° they are often not very good in positions of authority.° Virgos often choose professions in which they can work alone, and they are highly skilled in all kinds of handicrafts.° They are willing to give much of their time to helping others.

put things in order

power

objects made by hand

Harmonious signs: Capricorn and Taurus.

Astrologers advise people, telling them when the stars are most favorable.

Libra   September 24 to October 23

The sign of Libra is the scale—another fitting sign, since the strength of these people lies in their balanced° character. Libras particularly dislike anything that is unfair, and they try to do everything as perfectly as possible. They are kind and gentle with others, and never rigid°—they know when to work and when to play. They are often good at art and music.

Harmonious signs: Aquarius and Gemini.

even

not relaxed

Scorpio   October 24 to November 22

Scorpios are independent people with strong likes and dislikes. They are full of energy, yet they are able to maintain a complete control over themselves. Nothing seems impossible to Scorpios. They often choose to work in professions such as doctor or detective°—jobs that require overcoming unusual difficulties.

Harmonious signs: Cancer and Pisces.

detective

Sagittarius   November 23 to December 21

People born under the sign of Sagittarius are noted for their extreme curiosity.° Everything interests them, and, although they are impatient,° they will make a great effort to learn. They love the outdoors° and do well at all kinds of sports. Sagittarians often make good lawyers and journalists.

Harmonious signs: Aries, Leo, and Sagittarius.

the desire to know about things
not willing to wait

outside, away from the city

Capricorn   December 22 to January 20

Capricorns are people who move toward what they want in a sure and steady way. They are ambitious° and usually succeed

want to accomplish a lot

Step inside this astrologer's shop and learn about your future.

in doing whatever they decide to do. Capricorns take life seriously and defend tradition and authority. And because they understand the needs of others, they make good community leaders or diplomats.°

people who represent the government

Harmonious signs: Taurus, Virgo, and Libra.

Aquarius   January 21 to February 19

Typical Aquarians are extremely open-minded° about all things. They try not to judge other people, believing that everyone has the right to lead his or her own life. Their honesty and friendliness make them very popular, although some people think of them as being a bit eccentric.° Because they are patient and pay attention to detail, they make good lawyers and scientists.

fair

to behave in unusual ways

Harmonious signs: Libra, Gemini, and Aries.

Picces

Pisces   **February 20 to March 20**

give ...   appear to be

true

being alone

People born under the sign of the fish are usually quiet and gentle. They give the impression of being° cold and distant, but they are really sensitive and loyal° to their friends. The Piscarian is usually a dreamer who is little interested in ambitions or money. While some find success in acting, most tend toward more solitary° work, often in the other arts.

       Harmonious signs: Cancer, Scorpio, and Virgo.

[994 words]

Based on information supplied by the stars

EXERCISES

Vocabulary   *Choose the most accurate of the three statements.*

1. If something may or may not be true,
    a) it is probably true.
    b) it is possibly true.
    c) it is positively true.
2. If you tend to be serious,
    a) you are usually serious.
    b) you are trying to be serious.
    c) you don't mind being serious.
3. If you are a natural leader,
    a) you can lead others to be natural.
    b) you lead people to natural things.
    c) it is naturally easy for you to lead.

4. If it is not surprising to find that something is true,
   a) it is probably not true, surprisingly.
   b) you probably thought it was true, and are not surprised.
   c) you are probably surprised, but it is true anyway.
5. If you pay attention to detail,
   a) you are careful.
   b) you work on small things.
   c) you pay more than you should.
6. If you can't be sure of something,
   a) you want to be sure of it.
   b) you try to be sure of it.
   c) you aren't sure of it.
7. If a man is found in government work,
   a) he is looking for work with the government.
   b) he works for the government.
   c) he has found himself working for the government.
8. If you are little interested in something,
   a) you are interesting to it a little bit.
   b) you are interested in small things.
   c) you are not very interested in it.

little:
Adverb.

Take the Nouns.
Write the Adjective.

Word Families

enthusiasm → **enthusiastic**
impulse → **impulsive**

1. egotist - egotistic
2. energy energetic
3. harmony harmonious
4. surprise surprising
5. strength strenuous
6. independence independent
7. ambition ambitious
8. distance distant

Structures

A What do Aquarians think about? (their friends) →
Aquarians tend to think about their friends.

1. What do Taureans think about? (their jobs)
2. What do Capricorns think about? (the future)
3. What do astrologers think about? (the stars)
4. What do Cancers think about? (their homes)

5. What do Leos think about? (themselves)
6. What do Scorpios think about? (their dislikes)
7. What do Geminis think about? (the new and different)
8. What do Sagittarians think about? (the outdoors)

B Are they both impulsive and egotistical? →
They are impulsive but not necessarily egotistical.

1. Are Geminis both clever and stubborn?
2. Are inventors both enthusiastic and sensitive?
3. Are Cancers both imaginative and exciting?
4. Are Scorpios both independent and curious?
5. Are Virgos both careful and energetic?
6. Are Piscarians both quiet and eccentric?
7. Are Aquarians both open-minded and diplomatic?
8. Are Capricorns both ambitious and skeptical?

Horoscope

Choosing from the following words, make up a description, in at least four sentences, of (1) yourself, (2) a classmate, and (3) a member of your family.

steady	skeptical	self-concerned
ambitious	enthusiastic	generous
successful	afraid	understanding
serious	impulsive	clear-thinking
traditional	hard-working	careful
leader	egotistical	skilled
diplomatic	strong	helpful
open-minded	proud	fair
honest	orderly	solitary
friendly	systematic	perfect
popular	stubborn	kind
eccentric	clever	rigid
patient	exciting	independent
quiet	different	energetic
gentle	sensitive	dreamy
cold	changeable	curious
distant	loving	impatient
loyal	interesting	imaginative

Questions

1. What subject does astrology deal with?
2. If the stars are not favorable, what might a young couple do about their wedding date?

3. Where can you read your horoscope?
4. In what ways are Taureans and Cancers alike?
5. In what ways are Scorpios and Piscarians different?
6. Under which signs are good politicians born?
7. What signs are people born in January under?
8. How many people read their horoscopes in the papers every day?

---

1. Could any harm be caused by a belief in astrology?   **Discussion**
2. Why do you think many people believe in strange and secret things,
   such as what the stars say?

1. What importance does astrology have for you?   **Personal**
2. Do you think your sign describes you?   **Opinion**

23
Healing
by Faith

Where do doctors go when they get sick? Usually they go to another doctor. But what if the disease° is an incurable° one? Some ailing° physicians who cannot be helped by medical treatment turn to a woman nearly 80 years old, a woman who has never had any training in medicine. Other doctors refer their "hopeless" patients to her. For Olga Worrall has helped tens of thousands of people just by touching them with her hands.

Mrs. Worrall says she does not know why she has this unusual power. She is also not sure how it works, but she knows that it *does*. She has been able to heal° many people after their doctors could offer them no hope for recovery.

Do the powers which Olga Worrall and "healers" like her possess° really cure disease and stop pain, or is there some trick by which people are fooled into believing that they have been cured? Today, more and more scientists are investigating these unusual powers. They are finding that there may, indeed, be certain kinds of energy or ways of thinking that can change the way our bodies work—that can cure, or prevent, even cancer and heart disease.

Dr. Herbert Benson of Harvard Medical School has found

sickness or illness / not able to be made healthy
sick

cure

have

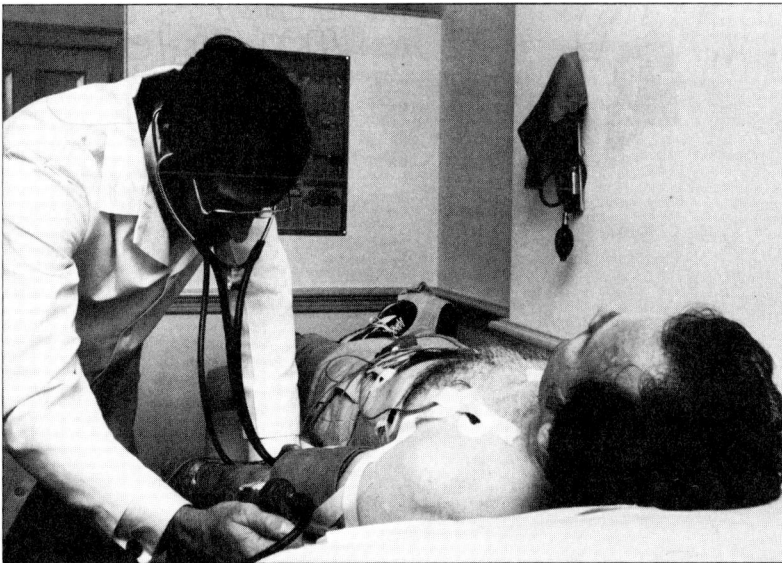

Doctors try to learn more about the body's natural defenses.

Present Tense.

that the brain and the way we think can cause changes in the chemicals in the blood, and that these chemicals can do as much to stop disease as some of the most powerful drugs. Dr. Benson is working to find ways to induce° the mental feelings which will make the brain release° these chemicals. His studies show that ten or twenty minutes twice a day of a certain exercise often produces changes in the body that help to fight certain diseases.

Dr. George Solomon of the University of California thinks that some of the "miracle cures" probably have a scientific basis° and are caused by the mind influencing the body and starting up the body's own natural defenses against disease. When people feel hopeless and helpless, they seem to have more chance of getting seriously ill. But when they feel positive and hopeful, the body's system for fighting illness can be much stronger.

Dr. Robert Becker's work has shown that all animals, including humans, have an internal° electrical system which controls the growth of the body and all its parts. Thus the brain can somehow speed up or slow down this electricity so that, for example, broken bones will heal faster or slower.

But Dr. Becker, a well-known surgeon,° finds that the electricity may go outside the body as well, and that this could be what happens when someone like Olga Worrall puts her hands on a sick person. It may be that the "electricity" from Mrs. Worrall's hands affects the electrical system in another person's body. Dr. Becker says it is not yet known exactly how these things happen, but he and many other scientists are trying to find out.

Of course, many doctors simply do not believe there is any truth to the idea of healing by "electricity." They feel that it is dangerous for sick people to trust a healer instead of their own doctors. Even Olga Worrall agrees with this. She will not accept anyone for healing unless that person is under the care of a doctor; she knows that her healing does not always work. At the same time, neither Mrs. Worrall nor anyone else has been able to explain why, so often, her touch is the treatment that heals.

Margin notes: cause, produce — let go of — P. Progressive — reason — Gerund — inside the body — **surgeon**

Try It Yourself

Physical exercise and (deep breathing) are two of the activities
scientists have found helpful in getting the body to fight off
disease naturally. Here is a simple exercise which you might
want to try yourself:

Wait at least two hours after eating and then sit comfortably
in a quiet place. (Close your eyes) and concentrate on your
breathing. Each time you breathe out, say a word—any word
you like; for example, "one"—silently to yourself. Continue this
for ten or twenty minutes. When you are finished, open your
eyes, but sit quietly for a few more minutes. Repeat twice a day.*

* If you are going to a doctor or taking any medicines, it is very important that
you tell your doctor before you begin doing this exercise, since it may have an
effect on how the medicine works in your body.

[730 words]

Adapted in part from *Modern Maturity*

Sit in a quiet place,
close your eyes, and
concentrate on your
breathing.

EXERCISES

Questions

1. How does Mrs. Worrall know that her power works?
2. What is the purpose of the breathing exercise?
3. Which people should tell their doctors before they begin to exercise? Why?
4. In what way does Dr. Becker think that Mrs. Worrall's treatment might work?
5. Why do some doctors think it is dangerous to trust a healer?
6. Why is it important to be comfortable and quiet when doing the exercise?
7. How does Dr. Solomon think the mind can help fight disease?
8. How is Dr. Benson trying to get the brain to release the chemicals to fight disease?

Word Families

The patients were without *hope*. → **They were hopeless.**

1. She couldn't *help* herself.
2. I had no *breath* left.
3. The doctor had no *power* to cure her.
4. The exercise had no *use*.
5. The body had no *defense* against the disease.
6. The sick man did not take *care* of his health.
7. He didn't *think* about other people.
8. The changes had no *meaning*.

Fill-ins

A *Fill in the blanks with one of these words: for, during, since.*

The healer has been doing her work _____ she learned that it could help people. But she only accepts patients _____ the time they are under a doctor's care. Sometimes she will put her hands on a patient _____ ten or twenty minutes. _____ this time, not a word is spoken, but _____ weeks afterward, there often seems to be a cure. _____ her treatment, a doctor may be present, in case the patient feels ill _____ a short time. But, _____ her work has become well known, most doctors allow their hopeless patients to go by themselves.

B *Fill in the blanks with one of these words: to, on, into, up, down.*

1. He was fooled _____ thinking he was cured.
2. Try _____ relax and be comfortable.

3. Start _up_ your body's own defenses by exercising.
4. Concentrate _on_ your health.
5. They went _to_ another doctor.
6. The patient was referred _to_ Mrs. Worrall.
7. The brain slows _down_ your body's electricity.
8. You will move faster if you speed things _up_.

Choose the most accurate of the three words or phrases.

1. unusual
   a) not ordinary
   b) very common
   c) one ordinary thing
2. miracle cure
   a) an unexpected cure
   b) a miracle, not a cure
   c) cure by electricity
3. internal
   a) inside the body
   b) the eternal body
   c) the intestines
4. deep breathing
   a) taking in a lot of air
   b) breathing from inside the body
   c) exercising while breathing

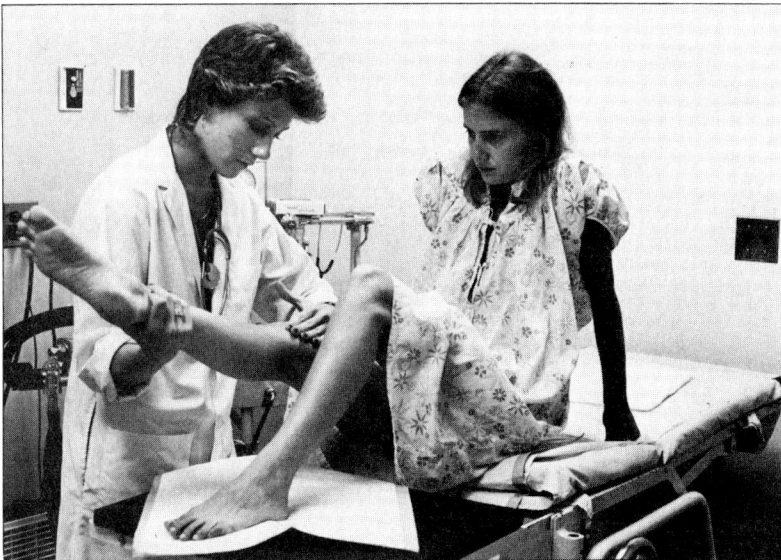

The body's own chemicals can often heal as well as some drugs.

5. ailing
   a) old
   b) sick
   c) healing
6. belief —> noun
   a) a way of thinking
   b) a chemical release
   c) the brain and its work
7. well-known surgeon
   a) he knows many people
   b) many people know him
   c) he knows many things well
8. somehow —> adverb.
   a) in more ways than one
   b) by doing something unusual ✗
   c) we don't know how

Structures

A That's Olga Worrall. Her job is to heal patients. →
That's Olga Worrall, whose job is healing patients.

1. That's Dr. Becker. His job is to find the electricity.
2. That's Dr. Solomon. His job is to make people feel hopeful.
3. That's Dr. Benson. His job is to stop disease.
4. That's a patient. Her job is to breathe deeply.
5. That's a healer. Her job is to put her hands on sick people.
6. That's the brain. Its job is to release chemicals.
7. That's a scientist. Her job is to learn more about drugs.
8. That's a doctor. His job is to give advice.

B When the patient exercises, it takes her twenty minutes. →
If the patient exercised, it would take her twenty minutes.

1. When Olga touches the patients, they feel better.
2. When the chemicals change, Dr. Benson knows it.
3. When the electricity speeds up, broken bones heal faster.
4. When these things happen, scientists are puzzled.
5. When people trust a healer, their doctors worry.
6. When you breathe out, you think of a word.
7. When you do the exercise, tell your doctor.
8. When he sits quietly, he helps to fight his disease.

C Mrs. Worrall touches the patient. → **What Mrs. Worrall does is to touch the patient.**

1. The lady repeats the word.
2. Dr. Benson studies the brain.
3. The healer accepts a new patient.
4. My body fights off the disease naturally.
5. The electrical system controls the body's growth.
6. Your mind influences your body.
7. A correct mental feeling releases the chemicals.
8. The patient takes the medicine.

Personal Opinion

1. Which would you rather be—a healer, or a scientist who studies how healers can cure patients? Why?
2. If you were very sick, and your doctor suggested that you go to a healer, would you go? Why or why not? What questions would you ask your doctor before you made your decision?

Discussion

1. Why is it important for scientists to study healers?
2. Why is it important to help the body fight diseases?
3. Why is it important for people to feel positive about their health?
4. Do you think it really makes any difference how people feel about their health?
5. Do you think people are really cured by healers, or do they just think they are cured?

Cross-cultural Topic

In your country, is faith healing or other nonmedical treatment of illness accepted? Why or why not?

The Cajuns

24

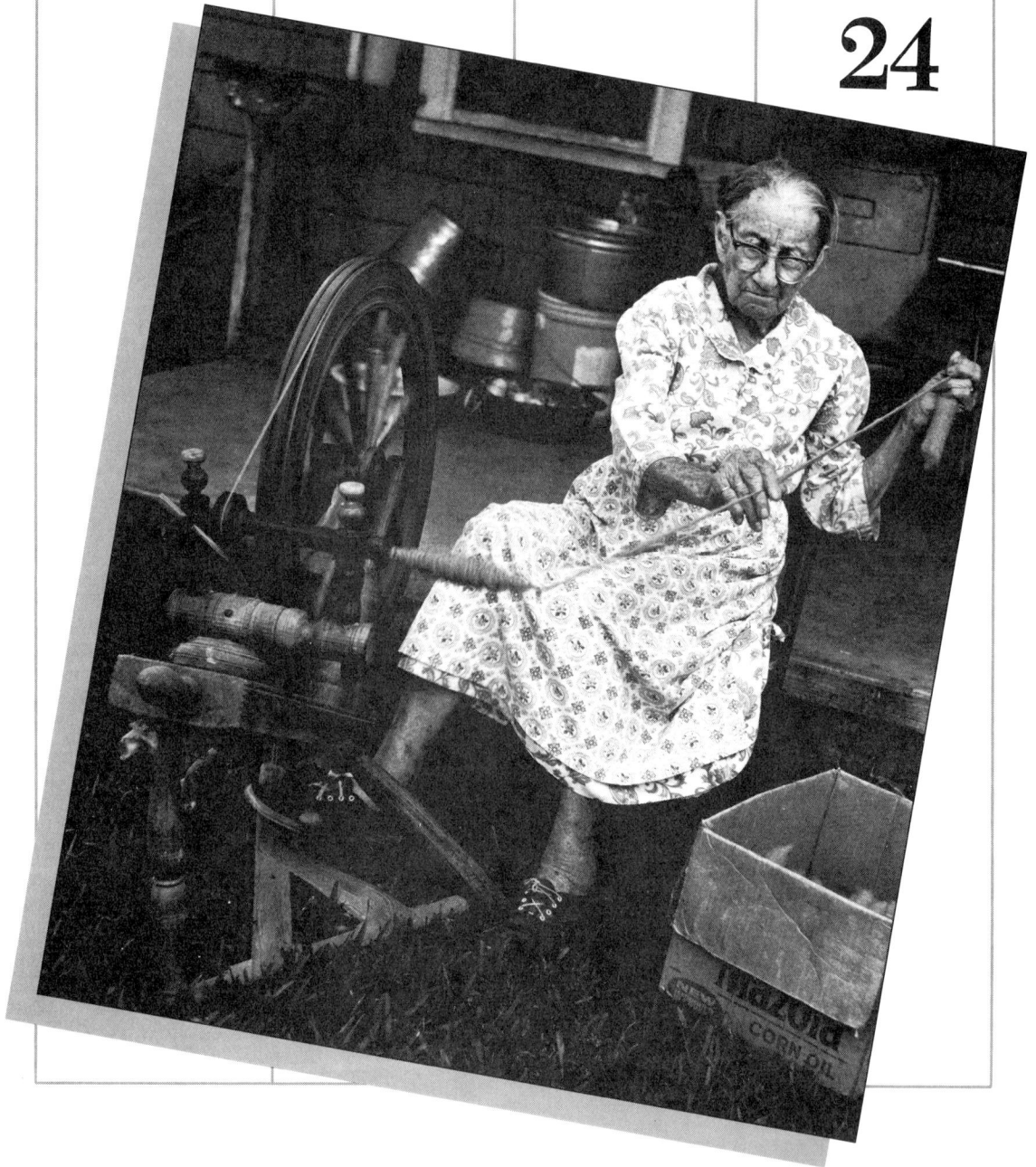

A story is told that describes the character of the Cajun (pronounced *KAY-j'n*) people of the state of Louisiana. The Cajuns are known for not telling strangers very much. In this case, it happened that a stranger asked a Cajun farmer how to find a man named No No LeBlanc.

The Cajun answered: "Walk on for about a mile, and on the right next to the big tree is the little yellow house where he lives."

"Thank you," said the stranger.

The Cajuns have been able to hold on to their own culture.

But the Cajun then said, "Wait. Did you say No No Le-Blanc?"

"Yes," said the stranger.

And the Cajun said, "I was wrong. He lives two miles in the other direction in a big brown house next to a small tree."

"Thank you again," said the stranger.

But the Cajun said, "Wait a minute. Are you sure you want No No LeBlanc?"

"Yes," said the stranger.

"Well, that's me," said the Cajun. "What do you want?"

common

This is a typical° Cajun story, the kind that people in Louisiana have laughed at for years. But now some Cajuns are tired of such stories, because they say they show them as foolish and not as good as other people.

unfair treatment

people who are different from most other people where they live

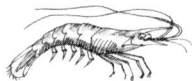

Actually, the Cajuns have a lot of political power in the state of Louisiana and have not suffered the same discrimination° that some other minority° groups in the United States have. The Cajuns have even been able to elect one of their own people governor of Louisiana. But, perhaps more important, they have been able to hold on to their own culture and have not changed to be more like the rest of the country. In fact, it seems that the Cajuns have had more effect on outsiders who have come to their part of southern Louisiana than the outsiders have had on them.

"The people who move here from all over—for example, those who work in the oil fields—begin to like the Cajun culture and soon become part of it," says Dr. Thomas Arceneaux of the University of Southwest Louisiana, an expert on Cajun history. "They want to learn French. They start drinking black coffee and eating shrimp° and oysters. They learn the Cajuns' joy in living—and it doesn't take them long."

shrimp

people from whom one is descended

The Cajuns speak French because their ancestors° left France in 1604. They settled in Acadia (pronounced *a-KAY-d'ya*), on the Atlantic coast of Canada in what is now the province of Nova Scotia. *Acadia* was an Indian word meaning "place of plenty." (The word Cajun sounds like and probably comes from the word Acadian.) The French settlers were happy in Acadia. But in 1755, during a war between England and France, they were driven from their land.

In 1765, about four thousand Acadians reached Louisiana—which still belonged to France. Their descendants now number about 500,000, living mostly in the flat plains and along the streams of southern Louisiana. When they first came south to their "New Acadia," most of the Cajuns worked as trappers, fishermen, or farmers on small farms. This was very difficult work, and there were many problems to overcome. Then, shortly after 1900, oil was discovered, and with it came money and advantages.

Today life is a little better for the Cajuns, though they are surely not afraid of hard work. They are still trappers, catching mostly muskrat° and mink;° fishermen, taking billions of shrimp and oysters every year; farmers; and cattle raisers. Other Cajuns work in the offshore oil fields, miles from land.

The Cajun quality spoken of most often by visitors to southern Louisiana is their joy in life. This is seen in the loud and happy dances in every town on Saturday nights, the many horse

muskrat

mink

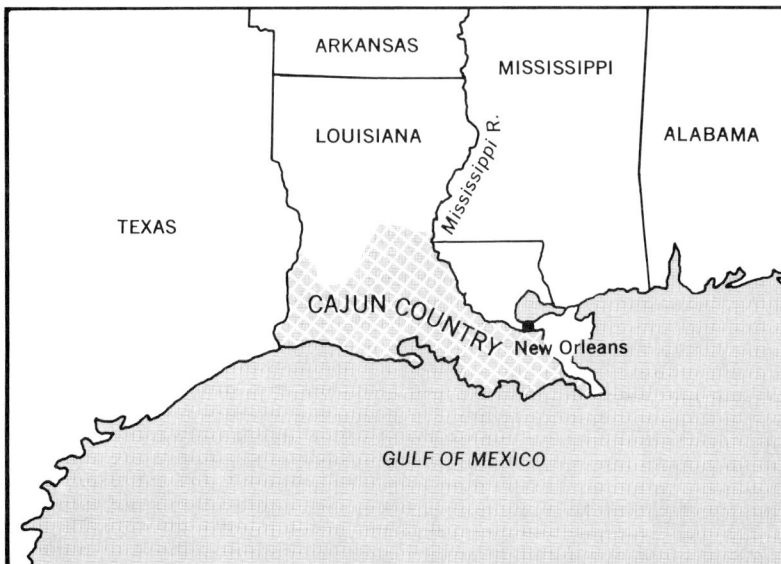

The Cajuns first settled in southern Louisiana in the year 1765.

races, and the Cajuns' love of good food and drink. There are festivals almost every week in the spring and summer in honor of everything from oil to jambalaya.° Yet the Cajuns' concern for their homes and loving families is clear. The Cajuns give a fine flavor to the mixture of people that make up America.

a Cajun dish made with seafood and rice

[596 words]

Adapted from *The New York Times*

EXERCISES

Vocabulary A *Complete the sentence with a word or expression from the article.*

1. I don't want to hear it again. I'm **tired** of it.
2. The Cajuns have kept their own culture. They have **been able** to it.
3. Other minorities have suffered more _____ **discrimination** than the Cajuns have.
4. One's great-grandfather and his family before him are one's **ancestors**
5. The French were forced out of their homes in Acadia **driven** from their land by the British.
6. Family life is what a Cajun is most interested in. Cajuns have always been **loving** about their families.
7. When the Cajuns left France, they first **settled** in Canada. **settled**
8. There are festivals for almost everything. One in **honor** of oil, another for jambalaya.

B *Choose the most accurate of the three statements.*

1. A stranger is
   a) a person who doesn't fish here.
   b) a person who doesn't live here.
   c) a person who doesn't like it here.
2. To discover something is to
   a) find it now.
   b) find it first.
   c) find it rich.
3. A person who raises cattle
   a) watches them.
   b) races them.
   c) owns them.

The Cajuns are a
French-speaking minority.

4. A flavor is
   a) part of a mixture.
   b) part of a culture.
   c) part of a country.
5. If a story is typical it is
   a) heard often.
   b) missed often.
   c) discovered often.
6. An expert
   a) knows things.
   b) helps things.
   c) clears things.
7. Almost every week is
   a) every other week.
   b) nearly every week.
   c) every two weeks.
8. A descendant descends from
   a) a father but not a granddaughter.

b) a mother but not a grandfather.

c) a grandmother but not a grandfather.

C   *In your own words:*

1.   How can someone have an *effect on* someone else?
2.   How can someone become *part of* a culture?
3.   How can a word *come from* another word?
4.   If something was discovered *shortly after* 1900, when was it discovered?
5.   Where does an *outsider* come from?
6.   Where do people come from who come from *all over*?
7.   How do you *honor* something?
8.   How do people *hold on to* their culture?

Structures   A   TEACHER: The Cajuns like to tell funny stories. →
STUDENT 1: **What do they like?** →
STUDENT 2: **They like to tell funny stories.**

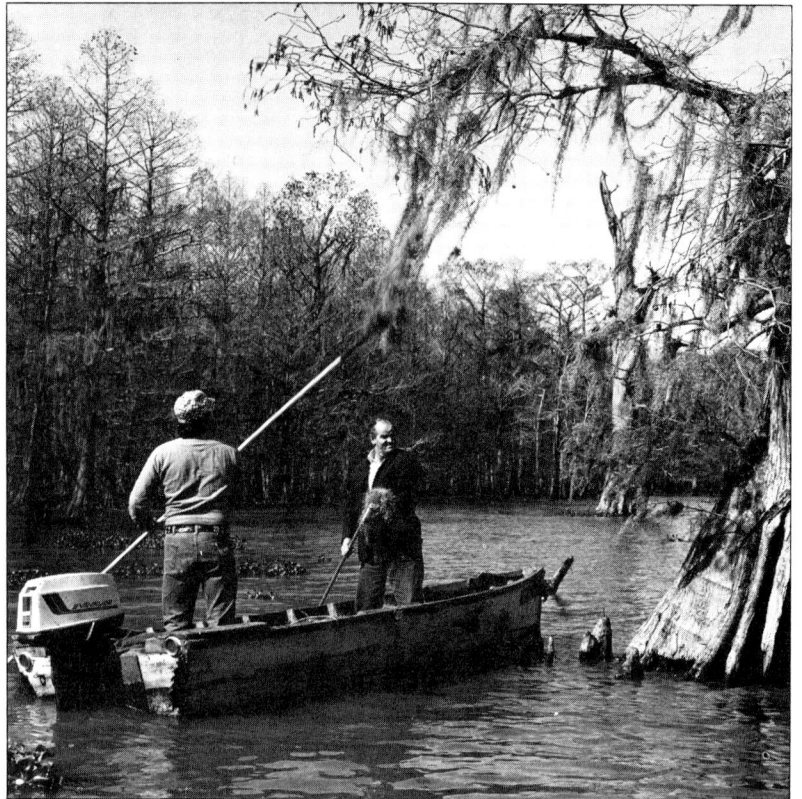

Many Cajun people work as trappers or fishermen.

1. The Cajuns live in Louisiana.
2. I want to ask some questions.
3. Bill is trying to find No No LeBlanc.
4. The Cajuns fish for shrimp and oysters.
5. They eat jambalaya because it tastes good.
6. Their real concern is for their families.
7. The Cajuns speak French to each other.
8. This week the festival is honoring mink and muskrat.

B Have they held on to their way of life? →
Yes, they've been able to hold on to their way of life.

1. Have they gained power in the state?
2. Have they elected a governor?
3. Have they made a living by farming?
4. Have they found work in the oil fields?
5. Have they continued speaking French?
6. Have they earned a little more money?
7. Have they raised cattle?
8. Have they gone to the horse races?

combining 2 simples sentences

C The Cajuns know many stories. Some stories are told in French. → ✳
The Cajuns know many stories, some of which are told in French.

*conjunctions
join
wich
becouse*

1. They did many kinds of work. Some kinds of work were fishing, hunting, and farming. *such as*
2. Some Cajuns work in the oil fields. Many oil fields are under the sea. *many of which*
3. The British and the French fought a war. During the war the Acadians were driven out. *and wich*
4. They have many festivals. Most festivals take place in summer. *wich*
5. The Cajuns have many amusements. Two amusements are singing and dancing. *such as*
6. Come eat some jambalaya. Half the jambalaya is gone already! *becouse such as wich*
7. The French used to live in Acadia. Much of Acadia has changed since they left. *but now much of this is change*
8. Their descendants live along the streams. All the streams are rich with seafood. *which are*

Questions

1. In what state do the Cajuns live?
2. Where was Acadia?
3. When did the settlers leave Acadia? Why did they leave?
4. What kinds of work did the Cajuns do when they first arrived in the South?

5. What is a jambalaya festival?
6. How do the Cajuns like their coffee?
7. About how many Cajuns are there now?
8. Why do the Cajuns speak French?

Points of View

1. Why do some minorities try to maintain the culture of their ancestors? Is it an advantage or a disadvantage to speak one language at home and another language in school or at work?
2. Some minorities manage, like the Cajuns, to get political power in certain areas. What advantages and disadvantages are there for the minority? For other people in that area?

The National Theatre of the Deaf

25

The theater of the *what?* This was the question people asked David Hays when he first suggested starting a theater of the deaf° in 1967. Most people could not understand how someone who could not hear would be able to perform in a play that would be entertaining.° But that is because most people did not know much about the deaf or what they could do. Fortunately, David Hays knew. Involved in other theater productions, Hays had seen a play performed by nonhearing students at Gallaudet College, at that time the only liberal arts° college for the deaf in the world. He was astounded° by the power and grace° of sign language, which uses the hands to communicate. He called it "sculpture in the air." Hays saw that the deaf are born actors— whose lives are a constant struggle to communicate. Although

Children can begin to learn about the deaf by watching an NTD performance.

many people thought it was a strange idea, Hays pursued° his dream. It took several years, with help from the federal government and private organizations, before the National Theatre* of the Deaf was established. But once it was, NTD, as it is called, attracted audiences everywhere.

worked to accomplish

"We must find ways," Hays said, "to let people know we are a theater *of* the deaf, not *for* the deaf . . . One of the things that drives us crazy° is that some of the articles written about us talk about a wordless theater. We're certainly not wordless. Sign language is speech. I can say 'My name is David,' then sign it . . . and then perhaps use a gesture.° Signing is a visual language." Of the troupe's twelve actors and actresses, ten are deaf. The two hearing performers use a combination of sign and speech. The result is that the hearing audience can listen to the dialogue° and see the visual language as it is expressed by the hands of all the actors and actresses. "Sign," says Hays, "starts from the toes up and includes the whole body." It produces a

drives . . . makes us upset

movement of the hands or body

words that actors speak

* In the United States, this word is usually spelled *theater*. However, the National *Theatre* of the Deaf spells its name with the form most often used in Canada and England.

The NTD's sign language is like "sculpture in the air."

combination of sound, movement, and silence that has a powerful impact° all its own.

force

Hays emphasizes that the goal of the NTD, like all professional theater groups, is to provide the best entertainment possible with the highest acting standards. The NTD repertoire° includes a variety of comedies and dramas by well-known American and foreign playwrights. "We are attempting, like any theater company does, to work with serious content."° To help bring this literary richness to deaf people in the audience, NTD performers use sign language of a highly expressive kind. "It's not the same language you'll see deaf people use on the street," Hays says. "It's intensified, broadened, enlarged." It is particularly effective on stage.

group of plays

material

Sign language is a very sophisticated° language. Most deaf people in the United States use American Sign Language, abbreviated ASL. ASL, different from English, is based on the visual concept° of words and has its own structure° and grammar. The NTD translates plays from English into ASL; then the audience hears the English and sees the ASL at the same time. Another form of sign language, fingerspelling, consists of a single hand shape for each letter of the English alphabet (see below). The NTD does not often use fingerspelling in its performances, because it is difficult for the audience to read such small finger

highly developed

idea / form

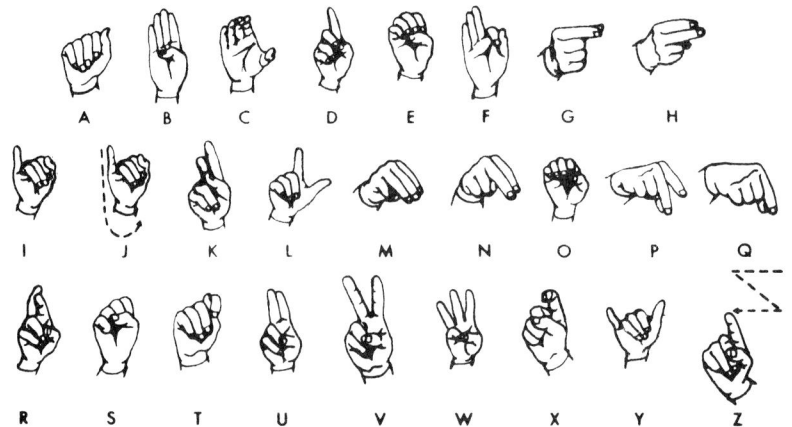

The NTD now has its own home base.

signs. But fingerspelling is a good first step toward learning sign language.

The National Theatre of the Deaf and its success have helped the public understand more about the deaf, and to realize that just because some people cannot hear does not mean that they are less talented or intelligent than their counterparts° who can. Deaf people watching the performances finally have a theatrical experience they can understand without help from anyone else.

other people like oneself

The popularity of the NTD is reflected in its busy performance schedule in America and around the world. Recently, it acquired its own home base in Connecticut where aspiring° actors and actresses can come to learn. The NTD has also inspired the creation of deaf theaters in other countries: performers have come from as far away as Japan to study with the American group. By bringing its unique° theater to the public, the NTD has helped ensure that the question "the theater of the *what?*" need never be asked again.

hopeful

unlike any other

[745 words]

Adapted from *Trends* Magazine

EXERCISES

Synonyms

Repeat the sentence, replacing the word or phrase in italics with one of the same meaning taken from the list below.

spoken words	grace	understand
form	gestures	spelling
enjoyable	deaf	got
mixture	appreciated	talented
question	words	intelligent
signs		

1. They find the plays difficult to *comprehend.*
2. Not all deaf people know English *vocabulary.*
3. There is a single hand *shape* for each letter.
4. The play is a *combination* of sound and movement.
5. We can listen to the *dialogue* and see the signs.
6. They *acquired* their own theater.
7. The *nonhearing* students also liked the play.
8. We wanted the plays to be *entertaining.*

Deaf performers from all over come to the NTD to learn.

In your own words, what is

1. a private organization?
2. power and grace?
3. speech?
4. a playwright?

5. ability?
6. success?
7. visual language?
8. literary richness?

9. sign language?
10. sculpture?
11. a struggle?
12. a troupe?

1. Why did people ask, "The theater of the *what?*"
2. What is the difference between a theater *of* the deaf, and a theater *for* the deaf?
3. What is the difference between ASL and fingerspelling?
4. Why do some deaf people have trouble understanding NTD plays?
5. How can a hearing audience understand NTD plays?
6. How can deaf people understand language they cannot hear?
7. What do the students at Gallaudet College study?
8. What is the difference between a wordless theater and a theater of the deaf?

A   Can deaf people act?   →
I wonder whether deaf people can act.

1. Can Mr. Hays establish a theater?
2. Can the hearing audience understand the play?
3. Can deaf people appreciate the performance?
4. Can we communicate by fingerspelling?
5. Can the hearing actors sign?
6. Can the NTD be successful?
7. Can they inspire people from other countries?
8. Can he say his name in ASL?

B   Can we learn the words?   →
It will take time, but I think the words can be learned.

1. Can we use gestures?
2. Can we help the public to understand?
3. Can we acquire our own theater?
4. Can we ask the question again?
5. Can we shape the letters carefully?
6. Can we express the visual language?
7. Can we combine sign and speech?
8. Can we include comedy and drama?

C   All the actors are working hard; the audience will enjoy the play. →
With all the actors working hard, it won't be long before the audience enjoys the play.

1.   More articles are being written; more actors will join the theater.
2.   We are working with serious intent; our plays will get better.
3.   They are communicating by fingerspelling; the standards will be higher.
4.   Mr. Hays is acquiring a new theater; the famous Japanese actress will come to study.
5.   Their hands are expressing their language; all of us will understand the words.
6.   Most people are asking the same question; Mr. Hays will answer it.
7.   He is attempting to teach sign language; we will all learn how to use it.
8.   The group is providing us with good plays; that deaf woman will go to the theater more often.

The plays combine sound, movement, and silence in a special way.

D He watched the actor struggling and said, "I can help him communicate." →

"I can help him communicate," he said as he watched the actor struggling.

1. He listened to the question again and said, "Never again will they ask that question."
2. He gestured with his body and said, "This *is* speech."
3. He started moving from the toes up and said, "I'm enjoying this."
4. He signed by using fingerspelling and said, "There are other ways of communicating."
5. He included a variety of plays and said, "We must have a larger repertoire."
6. He looked at the actress and said, "You are going to see a good play tonight."
7. He noticed the large audience and said, "They will see some unusual movements on stage."
8. He laughed at the question and said, "Of course deaf people act well."

Points of View

1. Would you want to see a play by the NTD? Why or why not? Which would you rather see—a play with hearing actors, or the same play by the NTD? Why?
2. "It makes no sense to have two languages for deaf people." What do you think about this statement?
3. Since fingerspelling is based on English, some people think that it, and not ASL, should be taught to deaf people in the United States. Do you agree or disagree? What do you think are the advantages of ASL? Of finger spelling?

Cross-cultural Topic

There are many special facilities in the United States to help people with handicaps—special parking places, telephone booths, entrances to public buildings, and so on. What is done in your country to help handicapped people? Do you think more should be done in your country? In the United States? What should be done?

26
Senior Citizens

With health care improving over the years, more Americans are living longer. Most of these people retire when they are about sixty-five years old, and sometimes they have problems afterward because they do not have much to keep them busy and interested. Many people and organizations are trying to change this by helping senior citizens° with their problems, seeing to it that they live comfortably and keep active.

senior . . . older people, usually those over 65

But there are some older people who never want to retire, and who keep on doing the things they love—and doing them very well indeed.

Famous Once Again

By day she looks like so many other older women out shopping, going slowly along on feet that move as though they hurt. She likes to ride the city's buses, often singing very softly to herself as she rides. If you hear her, listen closely, for the little old lady is the famous jazz singer Alberta Hunter. After twenty years away from the stage, the eighty-three-year-old singer is a star° once again, and, says she, "I'm the happiest woman in this world."

famous person

Alberta Hunter: "The happiest woman in this world."

At night Ms. Hunter is on stage, wearing enormous° round gold earrings, and singing the blues° for the people who crowd into the theater.

Ms. Hunter, who has loved music all her life, began her career° when she was only eleven years old. She ran away from her home in Memphis, Tennessee, because she'd heard that singers in Chicago were making ten dollars a week. Even though she was young and tiny, she was able to get a job, and people began to recognize her great talent. She traveled all over the world and became famous not only as a singer, but also as a songwriter.

During all those years, Ms. Hunter was very close to her mother, whom she brought from Memphis to live and travel with her. But when her mother died in 1954, there was a sudden and total change in Alberta Hunter's life. A few days after her mother's death, Ms. Hunter entered school and became a nurse. She gave up singing—forever, she thought.

For more than twenty-three years, she worked happily as a nurse at a New York hospital, where no one had any idea of her unusual past. Nor did they have much idea of her age. When they finally insisted she retire, they believed she had reached age seventy. "I was eighty-two," Ms. Hunter says with a smile.

She became terribly bored° and told some of her old friends about it. One of them suggested that she should go back to singing. She did, and she has been busy ever since.*

Flying High at Eighty-Two

The hills near the shore of the ocean a few miles south of San Francisco are a favorite place for people who go hang-gliding. The winds are usually strong enough to keep the gliders flying, and the sandy beach below is a safe, and soft, place to land.

---

* Alberta Hunter died in October 1984 at the age of eighty-nine. Recently, the hospital building where she had worked as a nurse was renamed the Alberta Hunter Memorial Building.

Eric DeReynier: "The thrill is worth the danger."

In the early afternoon, a dozen or so people gather, getting ready to jump into the air and fly out over the sea. One of them looks different—the only one with gray hair. He is eighty-two-year-old Eric DeReynier, who has been hang-gliding for over ten years.

Why, at his age, did he begin a sport that is considered quite dangerous? "Well, one day I came down here to watch, and it was so beautiful—just the gliders and the birds peacefully flying over the ocean. I felt I had to try it," he explains.

DeReynier has always been somewhat adventurous. As a young man, he went to China for what was to be a three-week vacation; he ended up taking a job and staying for six years, because "three weeks didn't really give me enough time to see the country."

Later, when he was in his late forties, Eric DeReynier rode a bicycle from San Francisco to Mexico and back, "for the fun of it." And at fifty he became a race car driver. "Now *that's* a dangerous sport," he says. "At fifty-six I was getting too old for it, so I quit."°   stopped

He feels quite safe hang-gliding. "There's no need to be afraid if you are careful to make sure your glider is put together exactly right. I exercise regularly and never do anything foolish while I am in the air. You can't let fear rule your life. The thrill° of this sport is worth the danger," he says—just before he glides off into the blue sky.

excitement

Always On the Move

There is no truth to the story that Mary Clarke is really a machine or a schoolgirl who happens to have gray hair. It just seems that way. However, there *is* truth to the story that once, while waiting on tables° at a Boston hotel, the tables were so crowded together that Mary Clarke had to go under them to get across the floor.

waiting . . . serving food in a restaurant

Mrs. Clarke has been working as a waitress for about forty years. At eighty, she is the oldest member of the hotel and restaurant worker's union° in Boston.

an organization of workers

On the floor, she seems never to stop moving, carrying trays° weighing more than ten pounds on one arm, while going around tables like a jogger.

tray

She says of the work, "I never get tired. There's nothing like walking to keep you healthy. The secret is that I'm from Prince Edward Island in Canada, and Canadians walk everywhere. It's so good for the body."

Mary Clarke got her first job as a waitress in 1938. Her husband had become ill and could not work. She liked the work so much that she kept doing it after her husband went back to work. Mr. Clarke is now over eighty also, but he retired from his job years ago, and now he drives his wife to work each morning.

Mrs. Clarke has no intention of retiring. "I'm having too much fun, and I meet such lovely people," she says. And what is the secret of her success? "You need two things to be a good waitress: a sense of humor and good legs." Mary Clarke has both.

Mary Clarke: "I'm having too much fun."

Hollywood's Secret Swordsman°

Have you ever seen an old movie where the hero, sword in hand, dashes° down a hallway, stabs° the villain,° leaps° up to the balcony,° and rescues° the beautiful princess? As you watched, what you didn't know was that the hero,° and the

runs quickly / evil person / jumps
saves from danger

courageous person

swordsman   stabs   balcony

villain, and probably one or two of the other sword fighters were not Errol Flynn or Ronald Colman or Douglas Fairbanks, Jr.; they were all the same person, Ralph Faulkner. When the camera moved in for a close-up, Faulkner stepped out and the star stepped in. "Otherwise, in almost every scene, I was fighting against myself," he says, laughing.

A master swordsman, Faulkner is a veteran of more than 140 stage and movie productions. At ninety-two, he's still teaching fencing to the stars of today and planning action scenes for future movies.

Faulkner started out, in 1921, as an actor. But he injured his knee while making a picture and began fencing° as a way to strengthen the knee. He liked fencing so much that he studied it seriously. He became so good at it that he earned a place on the United States Olympic team at Amsterdam in 1928 and at Los Angeles in 1932.

Returning to Hollywood, he at first resumed° acting but then turned his full attention to° planning action sequences.° He became a genius at inventing extravagant° swordfighting scenes. He also continued to teach serious, competitive fencers.°

"The two are not really so different as you might think," he says. "Both have the same objective,° and that's to hit the other fellow. On the stage or screen, things are done a little more dramatically. But the method is essentially° the same."

As for the future, Faulkner says lightheartedly, "I'm in this for the next fifty or sixty years. Retirement? It's not for me."

Lady of the Club

A 1,344-page novel about life in a small town in Ohio—begun more than fifty years ago by an author who is now eighty-eight years old and lives in a nursing home—is suddenly a "best-seller." Well over 250,000 copies of the book have been printed, and movie and television rights° have already been sold.

the sport of sword fighting

began again

turned . . . concentrated on / scenes
very complicated

competitive . . . people who fence to win

purpose

basically

permission to use

The book, called . . . *And Ladies of the Club*, takes place in and around Xenia and covers° the period between 1868 and 1932. The title refers to members of the local women's literary club, through whom the changes in the town's political, cultural, and social life are told.

deals with

When Helen Hooven Santmyer returned to her hometown of Xenia, Ohio, in 1929, she began the project that would make her famous. During the fifteen years she was away, she had graduated from college, worked as a secretary in a New York publishing company, taught English, become the head of the English Department, and written two other novels.

Miss Santmyer says that she wrote her book as a response° to another very famous work, *Main Street*, written by Sinclair Lewis in 1920. *Main Street* is also about small-town life, but gives a rather unflattering° picture of it. Miss Santmyer's book presents a different point of view. She says, "Not all small towns are wonderful, but I'd rather live in a small town than a big city, any day." She adds that she was surprised that anyone was interested in . . . *And Ladies of the Club*.

answer

not complimentary

Helen Hooven Santmyer: "I'm very suprised by all the attention."

There is good reason for her surprise. When the book was first published by a small company in Ohio, only a few hundred copies were sold, most of them to libraries. But one day Grace Sindell, who lives in Shaker Heights, Ohio, overheard a woman tell a librarian that . . . *And Ladies of the Club* was the best novel she had ever read.

Mrs. Sindell read it, loved it, and told her son, a writer and movie director, about it. After Gerald Sindell read it, he began telling other people. One of them said, "When I heard about how Miss Santmyer had been working on it for so many years, I knew that this was a book that had some wonderful things surrounding it. But when I read it, I was overwhelmed° by its quality. I sensed° that the book could have a second life and I wanted to help give it that."

This man took the work to Phyllis Grann, a New York publisher, who was at first worried about the book's length. "But not after I had read the first twenty-five pages," she said. "After that I knew I just could not *not* buy it."

Miss Santmyer wrote the entire book in longhand° at her house. Since 1976, however, she has been in poor health and has lived in a nursing home, where she made the final changes.

She is a quiet, soft-spoken woman and she doesn't seem to be too excited over her new literary fame. "I wasn't sure that anybody would want to read it. . . . I'm very surprised by all the attention."

Miss Santmyer said one reason it took her so long to finish the book was that she could only write part-time. "That was the trouble. I always had to earn a living while I wrote."

But she now feels that she has done enough work in her life. When interviewers ask whether she plans to continue writing, she replies, "Indeed° not!"

very surprised

believed

written by hand, not typed

certainly

[1953 words]

Adapted from *The Boston Globe, Modern Maturity,* and *The New York Times*

A *In your own words, what is*

1. the stage?
2. running away?
3. length?
4. a suggestion?
5. an action scene?
6. a rescue?
7. an intention?
8. a secret?

B *Complete the sentence with a form of the word "glide."*

1. A person who glides is a _____.
2. What he does is to _____.
3. The thing he hangs from is a _____.
4. While he is in the air he is _____.
5. The sport he enjoys is _____.
6. Birds also _____ over the ocean.
7. Last week, Eric and the other _____ met in the hills.
8. Then they _____ through the air.

C *Repeat the following sentences, replacing the blanks with words suggested by the italicized words in the first part of the sentence.*

1. She was *surprised* that anyone was interested in her book. But it really wasn't so _____.
2. Mr. Faulkner has no intention of *retiring*. _____ is something he never thinks about.
3. She keeps *singing* her _____ for her many friends.
4. Most people don't *recognize* Alberta Hunter, but others give her the _____ she deserves.
5. She became very *famous* in the 1920s, but _____ wasn't that important to her.
6. He *injured* his knee while making a picture. But that _____ helped him find his new career.
7. "Walking keeps me *fit*," says Mary, a perfect example of physical _____.
8. "I have no *intention* of retiring, and I don't _____ to slow down either."

Structures

A   She said she was the happiest woman in the world.   →
     "I'm the happiest woman in the world," she says.

1. He said he was not too old to hang-glide.
2. She said she was not going to retire.
3. He said he wanted faster service.
4. He said he still loved fencing.
5. She said she hadn't told them her real age.
6. She said she didn't want to keep on writing books.
7. He said he could always fight against himself.
8. She said her secret was that she walked a lot when she was younger.

B   *Repeat the following sentences, replacing the blank with a form of* let *or* leave.

1. _____ me have my fun.
2. Eric _____ (*past*) the younger gliders go first.
3. She has not _____ the nursing home since 1976.
4. She did not _____ anybody know her real age.
5. He _____ the star step in.
6. She does not _____ the hotel until her work is finished.
7. She _____ (*past*) Memphis to go to Chicago.
8. "Love me or _____ me," said the jazz singer.

C   *Add all the necessary punctuation to the following text.*

Alberta Hunter who has loved music all her life was born in Memphis Tennessee eighty-three years ago and she has been singing ever since then even today those who loved to listen to her in the past can find her still singing the blues the same sad songs she sang long ago before she gave up singing for more than twenty years during those years she worked in a hospital and nobody who worked with her had any idea that the old nurse had once been a famous star it was not until after she was forced to retire that she became bored with her life and so she was happy when some old friends asked her to sing at a party what a wonderful voice said a woman to her husband she's so much better than most of the young singers I've heard if she hasn't retired she should get a job on the stage again Alberta took this advice and now she is famous once again.

Sequencing

Number the events in the order in which they occurred according to the story.

_____ Helen Santmyer returned to Xenia.
_____ Gerald Sindell told people about the book.
_____ Miss Santmyer wrote the book in longhand.
_____ The books were sold to libraries.
_____ Helen Santmyer taught English.
_____ . . . *And Ladies of the Club* was published.
_____ The book became a best-seller.
_____ Mrs. Sindell heard about the book.

Questions

1. When did Miss Santmyer leave Xenia?
2. Why did Eric DeReynier stop driving race cars?
3. Who is the oldest of the five people in this article?
4. Who is the youngest?
5. Why didn't Ralph Faulkner continue acting?
6. Why won't Helen Santmyer write another novel?
7. Why did Eric DeReynier stay in China so long?
8. Why doesn't Mary Clarke get tired?

Discussion

1. "If people aren't forced to retire sometime, there will never be enough jobs for young people." What do you think of this statement? Is it better for young people or for old people to be out of work? Why?
2. What do you think about people who retire at about age fifty-five, or even younger? Are they happier than the people in this article, or not? Give reasons for your opinion. What do you plan to do when *you* get older?

Cross-cultural Topic

How are old people thought of in your country? Do they have an active part in family life? Can they continue to work if they want to? Are their lives better or worse than when they were younger? Discuss the special problems old people have in your country. What is done to help the old people?

The Indian
Land Claim

27

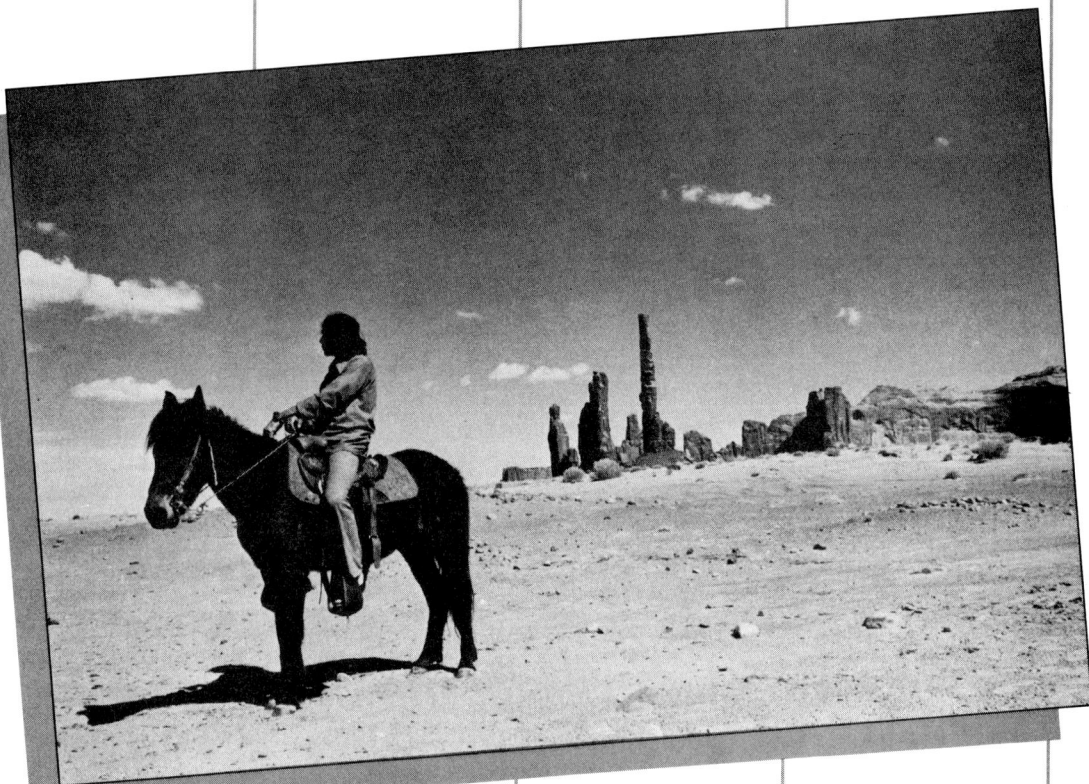

For thousands of years the American Indians lived and worked on their land. Then, during the eighteenth and nineteenth centuries, white settlers moved onto the Indians' land and began building their own farms and communities.

The Indians were forced by the United States government to move to uninhabited lands called reservations. The government promised the Indians they could keep these new lands, and treaties° were written which were supposed to protect the   agreements
Indians' rights. But as the nation grew and the new settlers moved farther west, these treaties were broken and more land was taken. What was finally left for the Indians often had poor soil and little water.

But, in the last twenty years or so, American Indians have begun to fight for their rights by going to court against the government. Very often the Indians have won. The courts have said that the treaties were promises made by the United States, and that these promises must be kept.

Reservation land is often poor for farming.

Often, the courts have ordered the government to pay the Indians money for the lands that were taken away. In Maine, for example, the Penobscot and Passamaquoddy Indians received $81.5 million. Some of the money goes directly to each Indian, but most of it is being used by the tribe to buy back huge areas of the rich forest they lost earlier.

In Alaska, the Indians and Eskimos whose ancestors originally lived there were given back forty-four million acres of land, a little more than ten percent of the state's total acreage. They were also awarded $962.5 million for their claims to the land in the rest of the state.

The government organized the native population into thirteen separate companies to distribute° the money to the people, who were living in two hundred separate villages. Each village also has its own company, which decides how the money should be spent and tries to make more money for its people. All this

divide among many

The Passamaquoddy Indians are buying back part of their land.

Eskimo life has changed greatly since the court made its decision.

has brought great changes to village life. People without televisions or cars have suddenly become owners of multi-million dollar companies and must make major business decisions.

Sometimes agreement on the Indians' rights is not reached so simply. For example, the Paiute Indians have a treaty which was supposed to protect their claim° to the water and fish in Pyramid Lake in Nevada. But over many years, much of this water has been used by nearby farms and mines, so that Pyramid Lake's water level has gone down and most of the fish have died.

demand for something that belongs to one

Everyone seems to agree that the Indians have rights to the water. But if the Indians win in court, what will become of the farmers and miners who have depended on the water for many years? These people have worked hard to turn barren° soil into productive ground. Now they are resentful.°

not productive

angry

Ted deBraga's father moved to Fallon, Nevada, in 1916. Today, his family works 1,500 acres of farmland. If the Paiutes win their case, deBraga could lose one third of his annual water supply. "Most farmers are unhappy," he says. "If the government takes the water away, they'll have to pay us just like they did the Indians."

Beulah Fajardo, a Paiute, has spent her seventy-five years living near Pyramid Lake and is now fighting the United States government in court over the broken treaty. "We've had a rough° life," she says. "Now I'd like our young people to have a chance we never had."

The courts are still trying to make a fair decision in this case. No one knows exactly what will happen, but it is almost certain that some of the people involved will have to suffer. There just is not enough water for everyone's needs.

[619 words]

Adapted from *Newsweek*

EXERCISES

Questions

1. Why did the Indians live on reservations?
2. How are the courts helping the Indians?
3. Why do the farmers and miners have rights to Pyramid Lake water?
4. How much did the Indians and Eskimos in Alaska have to pay for the forty-four million acres of land?
5. What is being done with the money paid to the natives in Alaska?
6. Why can't Mr. deBraga get enough water if the Paiutes win in court?
7. What are the Indians in Maine doing with their money?
8. Why is it difficult for some of the Indians to make major business decisions?

Vocabulary

A   *Complete the sentence with a word or expression from the article.*

1. The Indians have won many of their claims in the _____.
2. The _____ of the Eskimos lived in Alaska many years ago.
3. Each company must make a _____ about how to spend the money.
4. Because so much water has been used for farming, the _____ of the water has gone down.
5. With enough water, the barren soil could become _____.
6. A treaty is the same as a _____ which must be kept.
7. The government has been _____ to pay the money.
8. All the villages are _____ from each other.

B *Choose the most accurate of the three words or phrases.*

1. barren
    a) not on the reservation
    b) not good for growing things
    c) not Indian-owned
2. resentful
    a) full of water
    b) angry
    c) suffering
3. provide
    a) improve
    b) give
    c) belong
4. award
    a) improve
    b) give
    c) belong
5. acreage
    a) number of Indians
    b) land and water
    c) measure of land
6. annual
    a) yearly
    b) ancestrally
    c) total
7. huge
    a) rich
    b) original
    c) large
8. simply
    a) fairly
    b) easily
    c) directly

Retell this passage in the future tense. Begin: Ted deBraga's son will be a farmer.

Time Change

Ted deBraga's son is a farmer. His life is hard because there is not enough water for his farm. Some of his water is given to the Paiute Indians, but the government pays the deBraga family for the water it takes away. Even so, deBraga is not happy. He does not want to lose his water supply. But he has to continue suffering because there is not enough water for everyone, and the Indians have rights to the water also. This gives their young people a chance for a better life.

Structures

A   TEACHER: Do the Indians fight for their rights?
STUDENT 1: **Yes, they have decided to fight for their rights.**
STUDENT 2: **In fact, they insist on fighting for their rights.**

1. Do the Penobscots buy back their land?
2. Do the Indians keep their promises?
3. Does the village give the money to each person directly?
4. Does Mrs. Fajardo ask for more water?
5. Do the Paiutes protect the water level?
6. Do the young people watch television?
7. Do the farmers use the water from Pyramid Lake?
8. Does the government force the Indians to live on reservations?

B   He fished in the lake. He saw a miner.   →
He had been fishing in the lake when suddenly he saw a miner.

1. She lived on the reservation. She received a lot of money.
2. They fought the government. They won back their land.
3. The village bought more land. The government broke its promise.
4. He worked hard on the land. The water level dropped.
5. He grew corn. The Indians took back the land.
6. They moved to the reservation. The court ordered the government to pay.

The Indians want their children to have a better life.

7. He wanted a television set. The company distributed the money.
8. They used all the water. The farmers arrived.

C The government makes treaties. The treaties are broken. →
   The government is making treaties, which will be broken.

1. The Indians buy the forest land. The forest land is very rich.
2. The company decides how to spend the money. The money is distributed to the people.
3. Farmers use the water. The water is given back to the Indians.
4. The miners depend on the water. The water is more important for farming.
5. Water turns the soil into productive ground. The ground belongs to the farmers and the Indians.
6. Indians live on reservations. The reservations have little water.
7. The courts order the government to pay the Indians money. Some of the money goes to each Indian directly.
8. The Penobscots expect the land to improve their way of life. Their way of life reminds them of their ancestors.

---

1. Discuss the following: All the land should be given back to the Indians. It was their land originally and it was not fair to take it away from them.
2. How would you decide the case of the Pyramid Lake water? Discuss both the rights of the Paiutes and the rights of the farmers and miners. Do you think that the court decision, whatever it is, can be fair to everybody? If yes, how? If no, why not? If money is paid to the Indians, should the government pay it, or the farmers? Why? If money is paid to the farmers, should the government pay it, or the Indians? Why?
3. Does this story give you ideas of Indian life in North America that are different from those you had before? What did you know about Indians before you read this story?

Discussion

1. This story reflects a problem faced by one of the minority groups in the United States. What are some of the problems other minority groups face in America? In your country? How are they resolved?
2. Discuss the differences between the life of the Cajuns (Chapter 24) and the lives of the Indians you read about in this story. Also discuss the differences between the lives and problems of the Paiute Indians and those of the Indians in Maine and in Alaska.

Cross-cultural Topics

Photo Credits

CHAPTER 1   1: Wide World Photos; 3: Robert Anderson/Uniphoto; 4: Wide World Photos; 6: Courtesy, United States Department of the Interior/National Park Service.   CHAPTER 2   9: UPI/Bettmann Newsphotos; 10: © 1981 Peter Simon from Black Star; 11: Willim Dyckes; 12: Mark Antman/The Image Works.   CHAPTER 3   16: William Dyckes; 17: Courtesy, Wolf and Vine, Inc.; 18: Erich Hartmann/Magnum Photos; 19 and 20: William Dyckes.   CHAPTER 4   24: Peter Southwick/Stock, Boston; 25: Peter Menzel/Stock, Boston; 26 and 28: Courtesy, Dr. Ben Cohen.   CHAPTER 5   33: Wide World Photos; 34: William Dyckes; 35 and 36: Harvey Stein.   CHAPTER 6   39: Wide World Photos; 40: UPI/Bettmann Newsphotos; 41 and 45: Wide World Photos.   CHAPTER 7   46, 47, 48, 50, and 51: Harvey Stein.   CHAPTER 8   54, 55, and 56: Ursula Mahoney.   CHAPTER 9   61: Chicago Tribune-Universal Press Syndicate.   CHAPTER 10   67: Courtesy, National Marine Fisheries Service, NOAA, United States Department of Commerce; 68: Courtesy, Aqua Dynamics Corp.; 70 and 72: Courtesy, Cape Cod Chamber of Commerce.   CHAPTER 11   74: Dick Osborn/San Francisco Chamber of Commerce; 75: Courtesy, Golden Gate Bridge, Highway and Transportation Department; 77: Bill M. Barnett; 79: © Peeter Vilms/Jeroboam, Inc.   CHAPTER 12   80, 81, 82, 83, and 84: Courtesy, Preservation Hall.   CHAPTER 13   87: Peter Menzel/Stock, Boston; 89, 90, 92, and 94: Wide World Photos.   CHAPTER 14   96: Lynda Gordon/HBJ Photo; 97: Courtesy, Mrs. Corvia A. Christian; 98: From *The Descendants of Johan Frederick Brotzman and Maria Barbara Brotzmann, 1738–1968*, ed. by Mrs. Corvia A. Christian; 100, 101, and 102: Lynda Gordon/HBJ Photo.   CHAPTER 15   104 and 108: Courtesy, ASARCO, Inc.; 105, 107, and 111: The Star-Ledger, Newark, NJ.   CHAPTER 16   112: Aronson/Stock, Boston; 113: Barth Falkenberg/The Christian Science Monitor; 115: Laimute Druskis/Taurus Photos; 117: Ebony Magazine; 119: © Ellis Herwig/The Picture Cube.   CHAPTER 17   124 and 125: Courtesy, Department of Psychology, University of California, Santa Barbara; 127 (left and right): Yerkes Primate Research Center, Emory University, Atlanta, Georgia; 128: Paul Fusco/Magnum Photos.   CHAPTER 18   131, 135, and 136: Courtesy, *Millimeter* Magazine; 132: David Lyman/The Maine Photographic Workshop.   CHAPTER 19   138, 140, 141, 142, and 143: Courtesy of Terry Pimsleur and Company.   CHAPTER 20   146 and 148: Joseph Levy Photo/Yaddo Corporation; 149: Ellen Foscue Johnson/The MacDowell Colony; 151: Kathi Mitchell/The MacDowell Colony; 152: The MacDowell Colony.   CHAPTER 21   154, 156, and 160: © Dennis Brack from Black Star; 157: Inge Morath/Magnum Photos; 158: Photo by C. C. Pei. Courtesy, I. M. Pei and Partners.   CHAPTER 22   162: Courtesy of the Lick Observatory, University of California, Santa Cruz; 165: William Dyckes; 167: © Peter Paz.   CHAPTER 23   172: © Arthur S. Freese; 173: Paul S. Conklin; 175: Laimute Druskis/Taurus Photos; 177: Peter Vandermark/Stock, Boston.   CHAPTER 24   180, 181, and 186: Turner Browne; 185: Willa Zakin.   CHAPTER 25   189: David Hayes/National Theatre of the Deaf Photo; 190 and 193: A. Vincent Scarano/National Theatre of the Deaf Photo; 191: Melanie Barocas/National Theatre of the Deaf Photo; 194 and 196: National Theatre of the Deaf Photo.   CHAPTER 26   198: © Suzanne Murphy; 201: Ingrid Schultheis; 199: Wide World Photos; 203: Boston Globe Photo; 205: Toby Sanford/Wheeler Pictures.   CHAPTER 27   210: Ira Kirschenbaum/Stock, Boston; 211: Courtesy, TWA; 212: © Martha Stewart/The Picture Cube; 213: Courtesy, Pan Am; 216: Paul S. Conklin.

Copyrights and Acknowledgments

For permission to use the adapted and extracted selections reprinted in this book, the editors are grateful to the following publishers and copyright holders:

THE BOSTON GLOBE "Moveable Feasts Are Her Specialty," by Gloria Negri, February 12, 1979. Reprinted courtesy of *The Boston Globe*.

THE CHRISTIAN SCIENCE PUBLISHING SOCIETY "Aquaculture: New Hope for Food," (4/27/72); "Making It: Women Who Own Successful Businesses," by Jane Anderson (2/23/84); "Mobile Homes Help Ease the Housing Crunch," by Diane Casselberry Manuel (11/23/82). Excerpts reprinted by permission from *The Christian Science Monitor*. © 1972/1984/1982 The Christian Science Publishing Society. All rights reserved.

EAST WEST NETWORK, PUBLISHER "A Haven for Artists," by Ralph Fletcher. Reprinted courtesy of *U.S. Air* Magazine, carried aboard U.S. Air. Copyrighted 1983. East West Network, Publisher.

THE HALF MOON BAY STREET COMMITTEE FOR BEAUTIFICATION "The Pumpkins of Half Moon Bay," adapted from *The Pumpkin Book*, 1975.

HARCOURT BRACE JOVANOVICH, PUBLISHERS "Wasting Time at a Writer's Colony?—Let Me Count the Ways . . . ," by Jacqueline Berke. From *Shoptalk, the English Newsletter of the College Department of Harcourt Brace Jovanovich*, Fall 1983 Issue. Copyright © 1983 by Harcourt Brace Jovanovich, Inc. Reprinted by permission of the publisher.

JOHNSON PUBLISHING COMPANY, INC. "From the Bench to Brokerage Boss," by Alex Poinsett. Reprinted from *Ebony* Magazine by permission of Johnson Publishing Company, Inc.

THE LOS ANGELES TIMES "Wedding Sites: When You Hitch upon a Star," published January 5, 1983, by Dave Larsen. Copyright, 1983, Los Angeles Times. Reprinted by permission.

MILLIMETER MAGAZINE "The Man Behind the Camera," adapted from an interview with Vilmos Zsigmond, by Dennis Schaefer and Larry Salvato, from *Millimeter Magazine*, November 1977. Reprinted by permission.

MODERN MATURITY "Flying High at Seventy-four," by Ingrid Schultheis, February–March 1978; "The Healer Doctors Go To," by Arthur S. Frease, February–March 1975; "Hollywood's Top Swashbuckler," February–March 1984. All adapted with permission from *Modern Maturity*. Copyright 1984 by the American Association of Retired Persons.

NATION'S BUSINESS "Jogging Away from It All," by Jack Martin, September 1978. Used by permission of the publisher, *Nation's Business*.

THE NEW YORKER "Luncheonette," adapted from an article in *The New Yorker*, August 14, 1971. Used by permission.

THE NEW YORK TIMES "The Cajuns: A People Apart," by Roy Reed, May 9, 1972; "Fame Comes Again, to Alberta Hunter," by Leslie Bennetts, November 25, 1978; "A Family of Steeplejacks Keeps a Dying Art Alive," by Joan Cook, March 31, 1983; "Happy Ending for Novel 50 Years in the Making," January 12, 1984; "They Find the Right Face—Then Create a Mannequin to Resemble It," by Angela Taylor, November 28, 1977; "The Winning Ways of I. M. Pei," by Paul Goldberger, May 20, 1979. Copyright © 1972/1978/1983/1984/1977/1979 by The New York Times Company. All pieces adapted by permission.

NEWSWEEK "Land, Not Caviar, for Maine Indians," August 24, 1981; "Navajos vs. Hopis:

List of Words and Phrases Glossed

pass away	14	reverse	10	studio	18
pastry shell	19	revival	12	suburb	11
pattern	4	right (n.)	26	supplies (n.)	20
permanent	4	rigid	22	surgeon	23
picnic	14	risk	4	swordsman	26
piecework basis	16	roller coaster	13	symbol	1
planetarium	13	rootless	14	synagogue	13
pollute	10	rough	27		
pose	3	routine	20	talent	6
possess	23	run-down	12	technique	10
practical	21	rush hour	11	telescope	13
predict	16			thrill	26
prime	16	safety equipment	15	(from) time to time	15
professional	3	scared	15	tournament	6
pronounce	13	script	18	tradition	4
proof	17	sculptor	20	trailer	4
proposal	11	secretary	14	trainer	17
propose	8	seed	19	trapeze	13
psychologist	17	seminar	16	tray	26
pursued	25	senior citizen	26	treaty	27
putter around	16	sense (v.)	26	triangle	17
		sense of humor	22	tripod	18
quit	26	sensitive	22	try (judge)	9
		sequence	26	turn attention to	26
racetrack	5	setting	13	typical	24
rack	10	shallow	13		
react	18	shoot (films)	18	unflattering	26
recall	15	shopping bag	16	union	26
reflect	13	shrimp	24	unique	25
relaxed	3	skeptic	22	unpolluted	10
release	23	skyline	11		
repertoire	25	solitary	22	villain	26
represent	17	some time ago	19		
request	12	sophisticated	25		
rescue	26	stab	26	waiting on tables	26
resentful	27	staff member	16	waste	20
resident	4	star	26	watermelon	14
response	26	stereotype	16	way down there	6
resume	26	structure	25	wear out	8
retired	4	stubborn	22	witch	19